Cotswolds

AA

MINI GUIDE

KT-445-797

BOURTON-ON-THE-WATER

Author: Christopher Knowles
Art Editor: Alison Fenton
Editor: Sandy Draper
Cartography provided by the Mapping Services Department of AA Publishing
Internal colour reproduction: Sarah Montgomery

Produced by AA Publishing
© Automobile Association Developments Limited 2007. Reprinted Dec 2008

Published by AA Publishing (a trading name of Automobile Association Developments Limited,
whose registered office is Fanum House, Basing View, Basingstoke, Hampshire RG21 4EA;
registered number 1878835).

 This product includes mapping data licensed from the Ordnance Survey®
with the permission of the Controller of Her Majesty's Stationery Office.
© Crown copyright 2009. All rights reserved. Licence number 100021153.

A03906

TRADE ISBN-13: 978-0-7495-5584-9
SPECIAL ISBN-13: 978-0-7495-5691-4

A CIP catalogue record for this book is available from the British Library.

The contents of this book are believed correct at the time of printing. Nevertheless, the publishers
cannot be held responsible for any errors or omissions or for changes in the details given in this
book or for the consequences of any reliance on the information it provides. We have tried to ensure
accuracy in this book, but things do change and we would be grateful if readers would advise us of
any inaccuracies they may encounter. This does not affect your statutory rights.

Visit AA Publishing's website www.theAA.com/bookshop

Colour reproduction by Keene Group, Andover.
Printed in China by Everbest.

CONTENTS

INTRODUCTION

For many people the Cotswolds epitomise a vision of rural England – a collection of beautiful villages with mellow stone buildings, dotted with fabulous churches and wealthy country houses, and all set in a gentle landscape bisected by sparkling brooks and surrounded by evergreen farmland.

The whole region is protected by the Cotswolds Area of Outstanding Beauty (AONB), at 790 square miles (2038sq km), it is the largest area of Britain to be designated in this way. The name derives from the ridge of oolitic limestone to the west of the region, between Bath and Chipping Campden, whose wolds roll away to the east. Not all of it is gentle rolling hills. The Stroud Valley is deep and narrow with fast-running streams. The area near the ridge has some steep hills and fine views, such as those from Broadway Tower, Birdlip Hill and Cleeve Hill.

Sparkling rivers give the area much of its character. On the west it is bounded by the Severn, the source of much former wealth and a busy river today. The Thames rises in the Cotswolds near Cheltenham, and many of the pretty rivers, such as the Churn, Windrush, Evenlode, Coln and Leach that glitter through the Cotswolds are tributaries of this river. Much of the countryside is farmland, often broken up with dry-stone walls – a characteristic feature of this delectable rural area.

The Cotswolds has been a magnet for artists and craftsmen for centuries. Most famously, William Morris and many of the followers of the Arts and Crafts Movement came to live and work here. The Cotswold Woollen Weavers at Filkins, the group of artists and craftsmen at Bredon Hill and many others keep alive the ideals of quality workmanship and personal commitment espoused by the Arts and Crafts Movement.

The beautiful churches in the Cotswolds benefited not just from the exquisite work of the Arts and Crafts Movement, but also from the wealth that was generated from the wool trade in the 14th and 15th centuries, and the results are a delight to all those who visit them.

Yet it is the idyllic stone-built villages of the Cotswolds that give it its special appeal – their pretty cottages, well-kept gardens, charming pubs, local shops, quiet churches and village greens. In Snowshill, Bibury Castle, Castle Combe and Stanton the impossibly lovely buildings will take your breath away. And in Chipping Campden, you'll feel as if you have found the epicentre of this vernacular wealth.

The town and cityscapes are sublime too, as you'll find at Bradford-on-Avon, Corsham, Burford and Bath. There is an intimacy about these warm buildings which never fails to thrill and inspire visitors and locals alike.

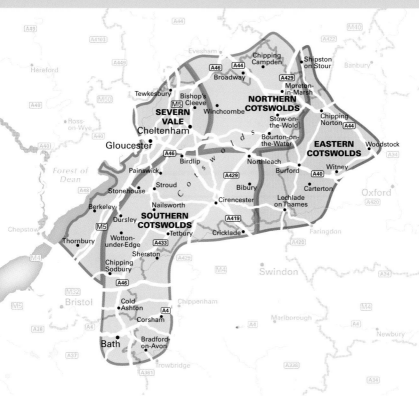

11

LECKHAMPTON HILL

ESSENTIAL SPOTS

Admire the panoramic views from the Cotswold edge, particularly from Leckhampton, Cleeve Hill and Uley Bury...walk part of the delightful Cotswold Way or along the Coln Valley...visit Stanway House with its charming gatehouse...climb Sandhurst Hill by the River Severn and look back across the vale...enjoy afternoon tea at the Pump Rooms in Bath or a beer from the local Donnington brewery at The Mount Inn, Stanton... experience the races at the Cheltenham Gold Cup...discover the 'lost' Saxon chapel built by Earl Odda...marvel at the world's greatest collection of waterfowl at Slimbridge...visit the grand palace of Blenheim, a gift from Queen Anne to the Duke of Marlborough...admire the church at Chipping Campden, perhaps the finest of all the wool churches.

1

1 Kelmscott Manor

Kelmscott Manor was home to William Morris for 25 years. From here, he led the Arts and Crafts Movement which used expert craftsmanship and good materials to produce simple, classic items, such as furniture, glass and textiles.

2 Church of St Edward

The Norman Church of St Edward in Stow-on-the-Wold has two ancient yew trees framing its north door. Probably planted in the 17th or 18th century, the trees appear to have grown into the walls.

3 Slimbridge

This Wildfowl and Wetlands Trust property, covering 120 acres (48ha), attracts more varieties of wildfowl than any other similar site in the world. The property was founded by the ornithologist and conservationist Sir Peter Scott, who also co-founded the World Wildlife Fund.

4

5

4 Hidcote Manor Gardens

When Major Lawrence Johnston the well-known horticulturalist acquired Hidcote Manor in 1907, it consisted of only the house, a cedar tree and a number of beeches. He transformed the grounds and created an elaborate garden that is generally considered to be one of the most influential gardens of the 20th century.

5 Blenheim Palace

The home of the Dukes of Marlborough is an imposing property set in a magnificent estate of almost 12,350 acres (5,000ha). Visiting the palace and gardens will happily fill a day. The palace hosts special events throughout the year.

Day One in Cotswolds

For many people a weekend break or a long weekend is a popular way of spending their leisure time. These pages offer a loosely planned itinerary designed to ensure that you make the most of your time, whatever the weather, and see and enjoy the very best the area has to offer.

Friday Night

Spend your first night at the Painswick Hotel in the village of Painswick, a hotel full of character, serving fine food in elegant surroundings. Alternatively, in Cheltenham, the Wyastone, Milton House and George all offer good value in a more central location. In the evening enjoy a wander around Cheltenham the 'Centre for the Cotswolds', a town of considerable charm and elegance, its handsome, wide streets lined with Regency-style villas and terraces.

Saturday Morning

If it's raining return to Cheltenham and keep under cover in the Art Gallery and Museum and the Pittville Pump Room, which has an imaginative costume exhibition; after lunch go to Snowshill.

Head up the escarpment on to the wolds through Prestbury and over Cleeve Hill. Stop near Belas Knap, one of the best-preserved Neolithic barrows in the country, to enjoy the view across to Winchcombe. Then visit the town, its handsome church

and Sudeley Castle and Gardens, one of England's most impressive historic houses with many royal connections; the entrance is down Vineyard Street. After Sudeley take the byways east and north and don't miss the various delights of Guiting Power, Naunton and Snowshill.

Saturday Lunch

For lunch The Plaisterers Arms in Winchcombe is a lively pub with good food and a large garden for fine weather. Alternatively, there are good village pubs in both Guiting Power and Naunton.

Saturday Afternoon

Continue via Snowshill (only visit Snowshill Manor just as it opens, to avoid the crowds) to Chipping Campden and devote at least a couple of hours to exploring the village. Drive to Burford via Moreton-in-Marsh and Stow-on-the-Wold.

Saturday Night

The Bay Tree in Burford, dating back to Tudor times, is luxurious with comfortable four-poster beds that have never left the building. The Lamb is a less expensive and an excellent alternative.

Day Two in Cotswolds

Your second and final day starts with a pleasant walk to two of the most charming villages in the Windrush Valley, before driving west to the medieval wool town of Cirencester, which is easily explored on foot. Round off your weekend in the Cotswolds with a visit to the Roman city of Bath.

Sunday Morning

If it is raining go straight to Bath with its many attractions, No 1 Royal Crescent, the Roman Baths and Pump Room and the Building of Bath Museum to name only a few.

If the weather is fine take a stroll east along the River Windrush to visit Widford church and Swinbrook village. Then drive to Cirencester via the A361 and the A417 through Fairford (the church here has some fine stained glass), or via the A40 and the B4425 through Bibury (picturesque but frequently crowded with visitors).

Cirencester, the most important of the Cotswold wool towns in the Middle Ages is most easily explored on foot and the Market Square is the most convenient place to begin a discovery of the town.

Sunday Lunch

The Swan at Swinbrook serves good lunches, whilst near Bibury, on the Fosse Way, the ancient Fossebridge Inn has a spacious garden by a stream. In Cirencester itself there are inns on the Market Square near the church.

BATH

STROUD

Sunday Afternoon

If time permits a late afternoon visit to Bath can be recommended, as the tourists are beginning to disperse. One of the most magnificent cities in Europe, Bath is known chiefly for its Roman baths and for the elegance of its Georgian architecture.

To see another side of the Cotswolds, drive along the Golden Valley towards Stroud and then head south through Nailsworth to Tetbury, with its charming Georgian church and Market House.

Northern Cotswolds

INTRODUCTION

Set in wide valleys run through with shallow streams, the northern Cotswold villages, such as Bourton-on-the-Water, the Slaughters and Stanton, are famously picturesque. Built using the local stone, they are the colour of honey, and many of these hamlets have barely changed since the time when the wool industry became the cloth industry and moved to the steeper southern valleys.

CHARLTON ABBOTS

Unmissable attractions

Watch the dramatic (and in reality, rather violent) cheese-rolling festival at Cooper's Hill on Spring Bank Holiday Monday...visit classic Cotswold-stone villages, such as Broadway and Chipping Campden...visit Snowshill Manor, a must for even the most museum-averse with its eccentric and eclectic collection of thousands of treasures, gathered together by Charles Paget Wade, as well as an Arts and Crafts-style garden...walk around Sudeley Castle set in beautiful award-winning gardens...spend the evening in Bourton-on-the-Water, called the 'Venice of the Cotswolds' when you can enjoy the attractive village and river in relative peace and quiet.

1

1 Sudeley Castle

The home of Catherine Parr, widow of Henry VIII, Sudeley was destroyed by Parliamentarians during the Civil War. It was fully restored in the 19th century and its rooms and gardens make for a delightful visit.

2 Chipping Campden

A shop housed in a mellow old building on Chipping Campden's lovely main street.

3 Snowshill Manor Gardens

The gardens here are designed as individual 'rooms' – each one is self-contained. The newer planting scheme has been designed to encourage wildlife.

BLOCKLEY

This handsome village, situated along the fast-flowing Blockley Brook, is less well known than many of its neighbours but has a subtle appeal undoubtedly worthy of attention. Blockley was a silk town and by 1880, just before the failure of the industry in the area, the six mills here employed some 600 people. Many of the weavers' cottages remain, the older ones towards the village centre, the 19th-century silk workers' cottages terraced along the northern edge. One of the old mills can be seen beyond a pool near the church, while the village, with its pretty mill stream, is dotted with houses of varying ages. A beautiful garden, Mill Dene, has been created around another of the old mills.

The church of St Peter and St Paul, with its Norman chancel, is unusually large, testament to its early status. Within is a Jacobean pulpit and some interesting brasses. There are plenty of good walks to be taken around Blockley,

Visit

BIRDLAND

Birdland was established by the late Len Hill, who purchased two small islands in the South Atlantic. These islands, part of the Falkland Islands, are inhabited by penguins and a considerable variety of other birds, some of which can be seen at Birdland, along with macaws, parrots and cockatoos, in varied habitats on the banks of the River Windrush at Bourton-on-the-Water. You can watch the penguins zipping through the water via the glass-sided pool.

which is blessed with a pub, The Great Weston Arms, a hotel and a delicatessen with a café attached.

BOURTON-ON-THE-WATER

The busiest honeypot in the area is this attractive village, watered by the River Windrush, which flows proudly along the main street beneath a succession of five graceful footbridges, earning for Bourton the title 'the Venice of the Cotswolds'.

BREDON HILL

A tourist hotspot, and to be avoided if rural calm is what you yearn for, the village does have a lot to offer in the way of attractions – Birdland is a sanctuary for birds, with a remarkable collection of penguins in stream-side gardens. There is also a Model Village (Bourton in miniature), a perfume factory, a motor museum, the Dragonfly Maze and a model railway exhibition, all within walking distance of each other and of the main street. Just off the main street is Bourton's church, St Lawrence's, a mixture of elements, with a medieval chancel, Victorian nave and distinctive domed Georgian tower, complete with skull on the exterior, a salutary reminder of our mortality.

Bourton can be best appreciated in the evenings after the crowds have dispersed, when a walk around its back streets and along the river is a very pleasant experience.

Just to the east of Bourton are gravel pits which, now filled with water, have become sanctuaries for waterfowl and make a very pleasant walk by following the path across Station Road from the car park.

Just west of Bourton is a group of interesting villages, Notgrove, Cold Aston, Turkdean and Hazleton, that are well worth a visit.

BREDON HILL

The landscape north of Tewkesbury, just within the Worcestershire borders, is dominated by Bredon Hill, 997 feet (304m) high, a huge Cotswold outlier (outcrop of rocks) shaped like an upturned saucer. The countryside of the area is, however, substantially different from the Cotswolds proper – building in stone is much less in evidence, and the landscape more in tune with the surrounding Vale of Evesham. The hill itself is an excellent place for rambling. In the autumn the lanes and tracks that criss-cross Bredon's slopes are thick with blackberries.

At its summit is Parson's Folly, an 18th-century tower standing amid the remains of an Iron Age hill-fort where a number of bodies were

BOURTON-ON-THE-WATER

discovered where they had fallen during some ancient battle, probably against the invading Belgae, some 2,000 years ago.

There are several villages of interest nearby. At Beckford silk continues to be printed by hand, while at Kemerton the footpath takes you through the exotic gardens of the old priory. Overbury, with its variety of half-timbered and stone houses, is one of the loveliest villages in Worcestershire. Bredon itself was immortalised in John Moore's affectionate story of mid-20th century rural life, Brensham Village, and in A E Houseman's poem, *A Shropshire Lad*. The village is noted for its magnificent 14th-century threshing barn with its aisled interior (National Trust).

BROADWAY

Broadway is almost synonymous with the Cotswolds and yet, with its wide main street ploughing busily up the lower slopes of the escarpment, it is hardly a typical Cotswold village.

Most of the houses that line the street in glorious array date from the 16th, 17th and 18th centuries. Some were inns, for Broadway was an important staging post on the London and Worcester route, following the construction of the road up Fish Hill in the early 18th century. The Lygon Arms, now one of the most famous hotels in the country, is a reminder of that period. Later, the village was the object of the attentions of William Morris, and other luminaries from the arts, including Henry James.

Most of the village can be discovered on foot and the completion of the bypass makes Broadway a pleasant place for wandering. Broadway's original church, St Eadburgha's, out on the Snowshill Road, is worth a visit. The town is overlooked by Broadway Tower, an impressive Gothic folly on one of the highest points of the Cotswolds. It is a steep walk from the village, set on the edge of the escarpment in a country park. There

Activity

THE COTSWOLD WAY

The Cotswold Way is a challenging long-distance footpath of 103 miles (166km), running between Bath and Chipping Campden. It takes about nine days to complete the distance if attempted in one go, otherwise it is possible to walk short sections of the route.

are exhibitions, and a telescope in the observation room gives wonderful views.

Nearby Buckland, within walking distance of Broadway, is a pretty village with a fine 15th-century parsonage, said to be England's oldest, and with some interesting interior features.

CHIPPING CAMPDEN

The loveliest village in the Cotswolds is a gilded masterpiece. The main street curves in a shallow arc lined with houses each grafted to the next but each with its own distinctive embellishments. As the name suggests (Chipping means market), Chipping Campden was a market town, one of the most important of the medieval wool towns in the Cotswolds. Chipping Campden then dozed for centuries until Edward Ashbee moved his Guild of Handicraft here from London in 1902. A few craftsmen continue their work today.

Campden's church, at the north end of the town, is perhaps the finest wool church in the Cotswolds, with a magnificent tower and a spacious, almost austere interior that contains the largest brass, to William Grevel, in the county. The Gainsborough Chapel houses the fine 17th-century marble tomb of Sir Baptist Hicks and his wife, who built the nearby stone almshouses in 1612, as well as Campden House, which was razed during the Civil War.

Among many fine houses in the village is Grevel House, on the High Street, opposite Church Street. It once belonged to William Grevel, a

Visit

COTSWOLD FARM PARK

At the Cotswold Farm Park, the home of rare breeds conservation, there are nearly 50 breeding flocks and herds of ancient breeds of British cattle, horses, pigs, sheep, goats, poultry and waterfowl. Newborn lambs and goat kids can be seen in April, spring calves in May, foals in June and cute piglets throughout the year.

wool merchant largely responsible for the church in its current form and who, it is supposed, was the original model for the merchant in Chaucer's *Canterbury Tales*.

Just off Leysbourne, which is the northern extension of the High Street, is the Ernest Wilson Memorial Garden, a charming little botanical enclave snug in the shadow of the church. The garden commemorates the eccentric plant collector who was born here in 1876. In the middle of the village, on stone pillars, is the 1627 Market Hall.

Chipping Campden is overlooked by Dover's Hill, from where – if you have the time and energy to reach the top – there are magnificent views across the Vale of Evesham.

THE GUITINGS

The valley running east of Winchcombe, following the River Windrush towards Bourton, is sprinkled with some charming villages. There are two Guitings, for example – the intriguingly named Temple Guiting and Guiting Power. Temple Guiting takes its name from the Knights Templar who owned the manor from the 12th century, and is a pretty village among trees at the edge of the stream. Its church is an interesting mix of styles and, although there are fragmentary remains of the Norman construction, the tower, pulpit and windows are 18th century, with stained glass from the 16th century.

Guiting Power, 2 miles (3.2km) to the south of Temple Guiting, is a comely village of stone cottages

TEMPLE GUITING

clustered around a small green, a secluded manor house and church.

The church to the south of the village, also once owned by the Knights Templar, has an exceptionally fine Norman south doorway. The foundations of a Saxon chapel have been discovered just to the north of the existing church.

Guiting Power hosts a small but significant annual music and arts festival in July.

HIDCOTE MANOR & KIFTSGATE COURT

Four miles (6.4km) northeast of Chipping Campden, in the hamlet of Hidcote Bartrim, is the National Trust property of Hidcote Manor, famous above all for its series of scenic and gardens with superb planting schemes that have transformed a comparitively mediocre 17th-century property into an inspiration for modern gardeners.

The 11-acre (4.5ha) garden, a mix of formal design and seeming haphazard planting, was created over the course of 40 years after Hidcote was purchased in 1907 by Major Lawrence Johnston, the great horticulturist. There are, in fact, a number of separate gardens, each created to a different design, and each producing different colours of flowers and shrubs, the effect heightened by the use of walls and hedges of copper and green beech, box, holly, hornbeam and yew, which also protect the plants, many of which are rare or unique, from the severe Cotswold winds. Within the hedges are the formal Bathing Pool Garden, the Fuchsia Garden, the White Garden and the Kitchen Garden as well as a less formal creation by a stream. In addition there are a beech avenue and a lime alley. Visitors can enjoy magnificent views of hill and vale from various points throughout the gardens.

Kiftsgate Court Gardens, near Hidcote Manor, are on a wooded slope from where there are views across the Oxfordshire wolds. Although less celebrated than

Hidcote, the gardens deserve a visit. The house is largely Victorian, while the gardens were created after World War I by Heather Muir. The terraced areas above the scarp are a paradise of colourful flower beds and shrubs, while the slope is covered in pines. Above the gardens are famous for a collection of old-fashioned roses, including Rosa filipes 'Kiftsgate', believed to be the largest rose in the United Kingdom at almost 60 feet (18.3m) high.

HILLS & COMMONS

The northern part of the Cotswold escarpment offer superb views across the Severn Vale to Wales. Best known is Cleeve Hill, whose summit, Cleeve Cloud is, at 1,083 feet (333m), the highest point of the Cotswolds hills and the highest, furthermore, in lowland England. This lonely windswept plateau straddles the way between Cheltenham and Winchcombe, distinctive for the radio towers that are starkly visible across the area.

Part of it is a municipal golf course, but most of it is ancient common, bright with gorse bushes on a carpet of coarse grass, as well as birds, orchids and butterflies. It is a fine walk across the hill to Winchcombe, via Belas Knap or Postlip.

Leckhampton Hill overlooks Cheltenham. Like many of the hills the length of the Cotswold escarpment, there was an Iron Age hill-fort and long barrow here, built by the Celtic La Tene people who arrived from the continent from about 300 BC. More recently, Leckhampton's quarries provided much of the stone for Regency Cheltenham. The tramways from the limestone quarries went directly to Gloucester Docks. Just below the lip on the west side of the hill is a local landmark, the Devil's Chimney, a pinnacle of stone left behind by 18th-century quarriers, and said to rise from Hell.

Just south of Leckhampton is Crickley Hill. In part a country park, it is a good place for family walking,

CLEEVE COMMON

with a number of trails of varying lengths. Here, too, are the earthwork remains of a fort used both in the Neolithic and Iron Ages. Cooper's Hill, southeast of Gloucester, is an almost sheer slope amid woodland.

On the slopes near Brockworth is Witcombe. In nearby woodland, are the remains of a Roman villa.

MORETON-IN-MARSH

A bustling market town strung along the Fosse Way in the Evenlode valley, Moreton is very much a roadside town, although its importance also depends on the fact that it has, uniquely in the area, a railway station; the railway arrived in 1843 and lines now extend to London.

Moreton is the perfect place for a wander, particularly on a Tuesday when the market swings into action near the Redesdale Market Hall built in 1887 in Tudor style. The 16th-century Curfew Tower on the corner of Oxford Street was used as recently as 1860 and has a bell dated 1633. Beneath is the town lock-up and

Visit

THE FOUR SHIRES STONE

This stone, just to the east of Moreton, is a striking 18th-century monolith surmounted by a sundial and a ball. It marks the original point of conjunction between Gloucestershire, Oxfordshire, Warwickshire and Worcestershire. Due to county boundary changes, however, it now stands in Warwickshire.

a board listing the market tolls of 1905. Just outside the town, on the Broadway Road, is the Wellington Aviation Museum and Art Gallery.

Near Moreton are some villages worth visiting. Bourton-on-the-Hill climbs the road to Broadway and has a nice pub and a handsome church. Bourton House Gardens are open to visitors and its 16th-century tithe barn houses an exhibition of contemporary art, craft and design.

Bourton's near neighbour is Sezincote. The extraordinary early 19th-century house built in Indian

Insight

CHEESE ROLLING

This strange annual ritual takes place every Spring Bank Holiday Monday on Cooper's Hill, just outside the village of Brockworth, near Gloucester. While its origins are obscure, it is thought that its current form dates back at least to the 16th century. The brave competitors line up across the crown of what is an exceptionally steep hill (1-in-3) next to a maypole-like flagstaff. A man dressed in a white coat and top hat launches the cheeses down the slope, to be pursued hell for leather by the racers, whose task it is to retrieve one of the cheeses before it reaches the bottom. Anyone who does so, and success is rare, may keep the cheese. Despite concerns about safety, there is local determination to ensure its survival.

style by Samuel Pepys Cockerell for his brother Charles, is worth, at the very least, a stroll by. Charles Cockerell is buried in the attractive church at Longborough.

Batsford, northwest of Moreton is an estate village with a Victorian church containing some excellent monuments while Batsford Park has an arboretum, and a falconry centre. To the southeast stands Chastleton House, a National Trust property, which is one of the finest Jacobean houses in the country.

THE RISSINGTONS

The Rissingtons, of which there are three, lie southeast of Bourton-on-the-Water. Great Rissington has, around its attractive village green, a handsome 17th-century manor house and a church with interesting memorials. Little Rissington, on the slope of the Windrush Valley, has an RAF base and a church set some way from the village itself, with an RAF cemetery. The village overlooks gravel pits, now sanctuaries for birds, close to Bourton.

Wyck Rissington, its 17th- and 18th-century cottages built around a wide green and village pond, is the loveliest of the three. From the 18th

century it formed part of the Wyck Hill estate, until the 1930s when the depression forced it to be sold. In the church, which, like several near the Fosse Way is dedicated to St Laurence who was martyred in Rome in AD 257, there is some fine 14th-century stained glass and Flemish wooden plaques dating from the 16th century. Gustav Holst, the composer born in Cheltenham, was organist here in 1892 when he was aged seventeen.

THE SLAUGHTERS

These two villages with unlikely names ('slaughter' means muddy, which they are no longer) are, like Bourton-on-the-Water, synonymous with the Cotswolds. The village of Upper Slaughter, partly clustered around the fine 17th-century manor (now a hotel) and the 12th-century church, is the more pastoral of the two. Beyond the church (which contains a monument to F E Witts, 19th-century rector and lord of the manor, who wrote *Diary of a Cotswold Parson*) the scene is absurdly picturesque – the forded River Eye bubbles in the shade of an oak tree below some stone cottages.

Lower Slaughter, about a half-mile (800m) walk away, is somewhat different in character. The River Eye is spanned by a number of flattish footbridges. The 19th-century corn mill, with its working waterwheel and steam chimney, has an interesting museum that demonstrates the workings of a Victorian flour mill. Among its collection is one of only three unused millstones left in the country. There is an award-winning gift and craft shop and riverside tea room, and free tastings of their hand-made organic ice creams in the summer.

SNOWSHILL

Pronounced, according to some, 'Snowzzle', or even 'Snozzle', this charming and comparatively remote village is famous, above all, for Snowshill Manor, a National Trust property from the Tudor period that once belonged to the wealthy and eccentric sugar plantation owner, Charles Wade. An ardent collector of anything that was crafted, he filled the manor house with his finds, living, meanwhile, in the Priest's House in the lovely terraced garden, without any comforts or conveniences and sleeping in an old Tudor bed. The fame of Snowshill Manor travelled far and wide, so that eminent people – John Buchan, John Betjeman, J B Priestley and Queen Mary who apparently said that the finest thing in the house was Charles Wade – were frequent visitors.

Snowshill Manor is one of the most astonishing and absorbing museums – with its Japanese armour, farm implements, musical instruments, clocks and toys, to name but a few – to all but the most hardened detractor of museums.

STANTON

Stanton has a fine collection of farmhouses and cottages, most of which were built during the 17th century, the golden period of Cotswold vernacular architecture. A village of absolute perfection, it seems almost to have been preserved in aspic; and indeed is regularly used as the backdrop for period films. It owes its peculiar 'frozen-in-time' quality to the man who bought much of the village before World War I, the architect Sir Philip Stott from Oldham in Lancashire.

Living in Stanton Court, he was determined to restore Stanton. This he did, introducing modern conveniences in the process, but ensuring by covenant that the more unsightly features of the 20th century were not to disfigure the village. A place to stroll around (making use of the car park around the corner of the Broadway road), Stanton's church, St Michael's, is delightful and well worth a visit. It has a handsomely slender spire, and a number of 12th-century features in the north arcade and also two pulpits, one 14th century,

STANTON

one Jacobean. It also has some 15th-century stained glass from Hailes Abbey near Winchcombe. The village's fine pub, the Mount Inn, is at its far end in the shadow of Shenbarrow Hill, with its Iron Age earthworks and magnificent views.

STANWAY

No more than a hamlet, Stanway is dominated by Stanway House and its 17th-century gatehouse with scallop shells, a reminder of the Jacobean builders. Just off the B4077 Stow road, Stanway House is reached by passing the St George and Dragon, a bronze war memorial by Alexander Fisher on a plinth by Sir Philip Stott, 'saviour' of nearby Stanton.

For a long time the gatehouse was thought to be by Inigo Jones, a theory that has been superseded by the belief that it is the work of Timothy Strong, the mason from the Barringtons whose family worked with Sir Christopher Wren on St Paul's Cathedral. The glow of the stone is breathtaking at sunset.

The house itself, a Jacobean building with medieval origins, has changed hands only once in more than a thousand years and definitely warrants a visit. Still inhabited by the owner, Lord Niedpath, whose aristocratic presence is much in evidence, the house wears an attractive lived-in aspect; and although it contains many items of interest and value, a less fossilised atmosphere is hard to imagine.

In the grounds there is a tithe barn, which was built about 1370. The old water gardens have been superbly restored and pride of place must go to the fountain, the tallest in Britain, which rises to over 300 feet (90m). The old brewhouse has been revived and the coppers are built over log fires making this one of the few log-fired breweries in the country. Several beers are produced, the most popular is Stanny, available in many local pubs.

Next to the house is the church with a Jacobean pulpit. Nearby is a thatched wooden cricket pavilion set on saddle stones, presented to the village by J M Barrie, author of *Peter Pan*. Barrie, a keen cricketer, was a frequent visitor to Stanway in the early 20th century.

STOW-ON-THE-WOLD

This windswept town, the highest in the Cotswolds, is at the meeting point of eight roads, and lies on the Roman Fosse Way, midway between Bourton and Moreton. At its heart is the old market square, surrounded by attractive pubs and coaching inns, shops and restaurants, for Stow's main claim to fame was as a prosperous and busy market town.

The square is not typical of the Cotswolds – its even, rectangular shape is more reminiscent of an Italian piazza, but without the arcades. Perhaps its exposed position on the wolds dictated its shape, to protect market traders from the wind. Leading into the square are a number of walled alleys or 'tures' which it is thought once served the purpose of directing the sheep towards the market place. The old stocks are still in place on the remains of the green in a corner of the square, while in the centre stands the Victorian St Edward's Hall, whose massive presence tends to overpower the more modest lines of the other buildings. Just to the south of the Hall is the medieval market cross, placed here as an appeal to the religious conscience of traders in their business dealings.

Overlooking the square is the imposing Norman church of St Edward, which in 1646 played host to 1,000 Royalist prisoners following the final bloody battle of the Civil War, which was fought in the vicinity of neighbouring Donnington. The church's north door is picturesquely framed by a pair of tree trunks while just outside the churchyard, on Church Street, is Stow's 17th-century school, now a masonic hall. A fine private collection of antique toys and other childhood memorabilia can be found in The Toy Museum in Park Street.

STOW-ON-THE-WOLD

NORTHS COTSWOLD BAKERY

STOW-ON-THE-WOLD

The Royalist pub, at the junction of Park Street and Digbeth Street claims to be the oldest in the county; unlike the many other claimants for this title, remains of wooden beams have been proven to be in place a thousand years ago.

There are a number of villages in the vicinity of Stow that are worth visiting. A 45-minute walk (or a short drive) from Stow to the north is Broadwell, built around a large green with a ford and overlooked by a fine pub, The Fox. To the west are the Swells, Lower and Upper. In Lower Swell, beside the River Dikler, the unusual design of Spa Cottages is a reminder of a chalybeate spring which was discovered here in 1807. It was hoped that the discovery would encourage visitors to come and take the waters, according to the fashion of the time, but the project foundered. At the rural hamlet of Upper Swell the road crosses a narrow 18th-century bridge near a picturesque mill, complete with an original 19th-century wheel.

If you are looking to keep children entertained, the Cotswold Farm Park, to the west of Stow near Guiting Power is a must. The creation of Cotswold farmer Joe Henson, the farm has a fascinating collection of rare British breeds. The aim of the farm park is to protect these ancient British breeds.

WINCHCOMBE

The capital of the Saxon kingdom of Mercia, Winchcombe is a town of considerable interest, with several legacies of its past that deserve investigation. There was an important abbey here during the Middle Ages, frequented by pilgrims who came to worship at the burial place of the martyred Prince Kenelm. Dissolved in 1539, all that remains of the abbey is the wall on one side of Abbey Terrace (behind which is private property) and the abbey church, now Winchcombe parish church. The handsome church, built between 1465 and 1468, owes its present form to wealthy local woolmen. Of note here are the 40 or so gargoyles, the Winchcombe Worthies, on the exterior, said to represent unpopular monks, a sign of dissatisfaction with the abbey at the time. A stone coffin inside is said to have contained St Kenelm's body and also a piece of embroidery attributed in part to Catherine of Aragon.

Along the main street are an assortment of interesting buildings (including the fine Jacobean old school on Abbey Terrace), as well as two small museums – the Railway Museum, with a collection of memorabilia; and the Winchcombe Museum in the town hall, next to the Tourist Information Centre, with a collection of police uniforms and finds from Belas Knap Neolithic barrow. Gloucestershire has very few castles; but Sudeley Castle, Gardens and Exhibitions, entered down Vineyard Street, is superb. Little remains of the original medieval castle, but of the 15th-century reconstruction undertaken by Ralph

Botelar, St Mary's Chapel, the ruined banqueting hall, the tithe barn and the Portmare Tower are extant.

During its Tudor and Elizabethan heyday, Sudeley was a place of eminence. Its owner, the ambitious Thomas Seymour, Lord High Admiral of England, eventually married Catherine Parr, the only one of Henry VIII's wives to survive him. She died here following childbirth and is buried in the chapel. Later, Queen Elizabeth I was to visit the castle on three occasions. A Royalist stronghold during the Civil War, the castle was severely damaged in 1644 and partially demolished in 1648.

In the 19th century, the estate was purchased by the Dent brothers, well known for their glove-making business. They began restoration of the castle but when it passed to their nephew, it was his wife, Emma Dent-Brocklehurst, an avid collector of anything linked to the castle, who ensured its present immaculate state. Still privately owned, the castle is surrounded by wonderful

WINCHCOMBE

SUDELEY CASTLE

ornamental gardens, beautifully sited beneath the Cotswold escarpment; conducted tours of the castle reveal a remarkable collection of furniture and paintings, all displayed with a studied nonchalance that is a delight.

Close to Winchcombe are a number of places worth visiting. A 45-minute walk, or a short drive, takes you to Belas Knap, one of Britain's best preserved Neolithic barrows with lovely views back across Sudeley and Winchcombe. At Toddington you can ride on an old restored steam train along a scenic part of the Gloucestershire Warwickshire Railway. There are future plans that the railway will eventually be reopened back to Cheltenham. The remains of Hailes Abbey, just off the Stow road, evoke the romance of the Middle Ages, while Hailes parish church, nearby, is of great interest with its medieval wall paintings and stained glass, a 15th-century rood screen and attractive woodwork.

Visit

SUDELEY CASTLE

Sudeley Castle, Gardens and Exhibitions has a number of gardens where visitors can wander through avenues of trees, shrubs, yew hedges and old-fashioned roses. Also within the grounds are a 15th-century tithe barn, a pheasantry and wildfowl area, an exhibition centre, plant centre, picnic area, shop and restaurant. Special events, including a game fair, craft shows and musical evenings are held in the grounds throughout the year.

Insight

VINEYARDS & TOBACCO

The slopes around Winchcombe were put to a number of uses apart from nourishing sheep. The monks from the abbey made wine, while tobacco was an important crop for some decades after the Dissolution of the Monasteries until the government felt that the competition did not help the new colony of Virginia and proscribed its cultivation here.

TOURIST INFORMATION CENTRES

Broadway
1 Cotswold Court.
Tel: 01386 852937

Chipping Campden
High Street.
Tel: 01386 841206

Moreton-in-Marsh
Council Offices, High Street.
Tel: 01608 650881
Information point only.

Stow-on-the-Wold
Hollis House, The Square.
Tel: 01451 831082

Winchcombe
The Town Hall, High Street.
Tel: 01242 602925

PLACES OF INTEREST

Batsford Arboretum
Batsford Park, Moreton-in-Marsh.
Tel: 01386 701441;
www.batsarb.co.uk

Birdland
Rissington Road,
Bourton-on-the-Water.
Tel: 01451 820480;
www.birdland.co.uk

Bourton House Gardens
Bourton-on-the-Hill.
Tel: 01386 700121;
www.bourtonhouse.com

Bredon Barn
Bredon. Tel: 01451 844257;
www.nationaltrust.org.uk

Broadway Tower
Country Park
Broadway. Tel: 01386 852390;
www.broadwaytower.co.uk

Chastleton House
nr Moreton-in-Marsh.
Tel:01608 674355;
www.nationaltrust.org.uk

Cotswold Falconry Centre
Batsford Park, Moreton-in-Marsh.
Tel: 01386 701043;
www.cotswold-falconry.co.uk

Cotswold Farm Park
Guiting Power.
Tel: 01451 850307;
www.cotswoldfarmpark.co.uk

Cotswold Motoring Museum, Toy Collection & Village Life Exhibition
The Old Mill, Bourton-on-the-Water.
Tel: 01451 821255;
www.cotswold-motor-museum.com

Cotswold Perfumery
Bourton-on-the-Water.
Tel: 01451 820698;
www.cotswold-perfumery.co.uk

Domestic Fowl Trust
Honeybourne, nr Weston-sub-Edge.
Tel: 01386 833083;
www.domesticfowltrust.co.uk

**Gloucestershire & Warwickshire
Railway**
Toddington Station, Winchcombe.
Tel: 01242 621405; www.gwsr.com

Hailes Abbey
Winchcombe. Tel: 01242 602398;
www.english-heritage.org.uk

Hidcote Manor
Mickleton. Tel: 01386 438333;
www.nationaltrust.org.uk

Kiftsgate Court
Mickleton. Tel: 01386 438777;
www.kiftsgate.co.uk

Mill Dene Garden
Blockley. Tel: 01386 700457;
www.milldenegarden.co.uk

**Model Railway Exhibition Bourton-on-
the-Water.**
Tel: 01451 820686;
www.bourtonmodelrailway.co.uk

Model Village
Old New Inn, Main Street,
Bourton-on-the-Water.
Tel: 01451 820467;
www.theoldnewinn.co.uk

Old Mill Museum
Mill Lane, Lower Slaughter.
Tel: 01451 820052;
www.oldmill-lowerslaughter.com

Railway Museum
Gloucester Street, Winchcombe.
Tel: 01242 609305

Sezincote
Moreton-in-Marsh. Tel: 01386 700444

Snowshill Manor
Tel: 01386 852410;
www.nationaltrust.org.uk

Stanway House
Tel: 01386 584469;
www.stanwayfountain.co.uk

Sudeley Castle
Winchcombe. Tel: 01242 602308;
www.sudeleycastle.co.uk

**Wellington Aviation Museum & Art
Gallery**
Broadway Road, Moreton-in-Marsh.
Tel: 01608 650323;
www.wellingtonaviation.org

71

Winchcombe Folk & Police Museum
Old Town Hall, Winchcombe.
Tel: 01242 609151;
www.sunloch.demon.co.uk/
museum.htm

Winchcombe Pottery
Broadway Road. Tel: 01242 602462;
www.winchcombepottery.co.uk

FOR CHILDREN
Cotswold Farm Park
Nr. Guiting Power.
Tel: 01451 850307;
www.cotswoldfarmpark.co.uk

Dragonfly Maze
Bourton-on-the-Water.
Tel: 01451 822251

Giffords Circus
Tel: 01242 572573;
www.giffordscircus.com

Toy Museum
Park Street, Stow-on-the-Wold.
Tel: 01451 830159;
www.thetoymuseum.co.uk

SHOPPING
Moreton-in-Marsh
Market in town centre, Tue.

LOCAL SPECIALITIES
Pottery
Bredon Pottery
Bredon. Tel:01684 773417;
www.bredonpottery.co.uk
Winchcombe Pottery, Broadway Road,
Winchcombe. Tel: 01242 602462;
www.winchcombepottery.co.uk

Silk Printing
Beckford Silk, Ashton Road, Beckford
near Tewkesbury.
Tel: 01386 881507;
www.beckfordsilk.co.uk

Silverware
David Hart, Sheep Street, Chipping
Campden. Tel: 01386 841100;
www.hartsilversmiths.co.uk

SPORTS & ACTIVITIES
ANGLING
Aston Magna Pool
Permits from Batsford Estate Office.
Tel: 01608 650425

ARCHERY
Aston Magna
Rob Ireland Activity Days
Tel: 01368 701683;
www.robireland.co.uk

CLAY PIGEON SHOOTING
Coberley
Chatcombe Estate Shooting School,
Chatcombe, Coberley.
Tel: 01242 870391
Moreton-in-Marsh
Rob Ireland Activity Days, Aston Magna.
Tel: 01368 701683;
www.robireland.co.uk

COUNTRY PARKS & NATURE RESERVES
Broadway Tower Country Park, Crickley
Hill, near Leckhampton.
Tel: 01386 852390;
www.broadwaytower.co.uk

CYCLING
Hartwells Cycle Hire, High Street,
Bourton-on-the-Water.
Tel:01451 820405;
www.hartwells.supanet.com

GUIDED WALKS
Cotswolds Walking Holidays Ltd,
30 Imperial Square, Cheltenham.
Tel: 01242 254353;
www.cotswoldwalks.com
The Voluntary Wardens
Tel: 01451 862000;
www.cotswoldsaonb.org.uk

HILL-CLIMBS
Motor speed hill-climbs at Prescott,
2 miles (3.2km) west of Winchcombe.
Bugatti Owners' Club.
Tel: 01242 673136; www.bugatti.co.uk

ANNUAL EVENTS & CUSTOMS
Chipping Campden
Dover's Hill Olympick Games and
Scuttlebrook Wake, Spring Bank
Holiday; www.olimpickgames.co.uk
Cooper's Hill
Cheese Rolling, Spring Bank Holiday
Mon.
Cranham
Annual Feast and Ox Roast, Aug.
Guiting Power
Festival of Music and Arts, Jul.
Moreton-in-Marsh
Agricultural Show, Sep.
Winchcombe
Sudeley Castle events.
Tel: 01242 602308

73

TEA ROOMS

The Mad Hatter
Riverside, Bourton-on-the-Water,
GL54 2BX
Tel: 01451 821508
www.the-mad-hatter-tearoom.co.uk
This lovely 18th-century building beside
the River Windrush is a treat. Enjoy
their cream teas, home-made cakes
and lovely garden.

Tisanes
21 The Green, Broadway, WR12 7AA
Tel: 01386 853296
www.tisanes-tearooms.co.uk
They serve wonderful cream teas,
as well as an unusual and extensive
variety of sandwiches and lunches in
this pretty 17th-century stone building
on the High Street.

The Marshmallow
High Street, Moreton-in-Marsh,
GL56 0AT
Tel: 01608 651536
Behind the attractive frontage covered
in Virginia creeper, is a stone-flagged
courtyard with tables and hanging
baskets – the ideal setting for tea.

Badgers Hall
High Street, Chipping Campden,
GL55 6HB
Tel: 01386 840839
www.badgershall.com
A true taste of the Cotswolds: the
building is 15th century, honey-
coloured stone with exposed oak
beams, mullioned windows and open
fireplaces. Home-made cakes, scones
and pastries are freshly baked on the
premises using local produce. They
also have charming rooms available.

Juri's Tearoom
High Street, Winchcombe, GL54 5LJ
Tel: 01242 602469
www.juris-tearoom.co.uk
On the High Street of this lovely village,
Juri's traditional stone tea room is run
by a Japanese family who are dedicated
to maintaining high standards. Their
freshly made cakes are first class. The
patio garden in warm weather and the
conservatory are delightful.

Eight Bells

Church Street, Chipping Campden,
GL55 6JG
Tel: 01386 840371
www.eightbellsinn.co.uk

This is the oldest inn in Chipping
Campden and is near the famous
church. It has two cosy bars, a smart
dining room and a very pleasant
terrace at the back. They serve a good
range of local food at lunchtime and in
the evenings.

The Lamb Inn

Great Rissington, GL54 2LP
Tel: 01451 820388
www.thelambinn.com

This rambling Cotswold stone inn dates
back 300 years. It now offers modern-
style home-cooked food with traditional
beers and wine. Among its attractions
is part of a Wellington bomber, which
crashed in the garden in 1943.

The White Hart

High Street, Winchcombe, GL54 5LJ
Tel: 01242 602359
www.the-white-hart-inn.com

Crisp Scandinavian style blends with
this 16th-century coaching inn to
make an unusual combination, but
one that works. The food may be pizza,
Scandinavian hotdog or excellent fish,
but it is all good quality, and the local
beers are good.

Horse and Groom Inn

Upper Oddington, GL56 0XH
Tel: 01451 830584
www.horseandgroom.uk.com

Aiming to serve the best pub food
in the Cotswolds, this immaculate
16th-century stone pub changes the
specials board twice daily. The food is
imaginative, the beers are local and the
setting is glorious.

Severn Vale

ASHLEWORTH

BERKELEY

CHELTENHAM

DEERHURST & ODDA'S CHAPEL

GLOUCESTER

SLIMBRIDGE

TEWKESBURY

THORNBURY

INTRODUCTION

The Severn Vale lies between the Cotswold escarpment and the River Severn, Britain's longest river; along the banks of the Severn are the flat fertile lands of the Vale of Berkeley. The Severn Vale, with its brick houses and half-timbered cottages, is quite different in character from the mellow stone villages of the wolds, yet wold and vale are closely linked – they both, to a large extent, belong to Gloucestershire and many of the historical events that have shaped the county have taken place in the towns of the vale and wold – consequently, they are almost inseparable.

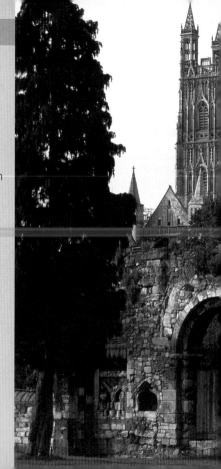

Unmissable attractions

Explore Cheltenham, a Regency delight with elegant architecture, antique shops, the Pump Rooms, an art gallery and museum to visit…or go shopping in Gloucester, which also has a thousand-year-old cathedral, as well as an Antiques Centre and the National Waterways Museum…or for another ancient gem visit Odda's Chapel at Deerhurst, which is a complete Saxon chapel…nature lovers should head for the Wildfowl and Wetlands Trust at Slimbridge which, impressively, has one of the greatest collections of waterfowl in the world…wander around Berkeley Castle and enjoy its rich history, dungeons and works of art.

1

1 Slimbridge Wildfowl Trust
The Wildfowl Trust has the world's largest and most varied collection of wildfowl. There is also a tropical house with humming birds.

2 Gloucester Cathedral
There is much of interest to see here. Apart from what will interest adults, children might be interested to know that the cloisters were one of the locations in the first two Harry Potter films.

3 Odda's Chapel
The chapel at Deerhurst was built in 1056 by Earl Odda in memory of his brother Aelfric, who had died at Deerhurst three years previously. A replica of the Odda Stone set into the wall tells the story of the chapel's construction.

ASHLEWORTH

Although this little village lies on the west bank of the Severn, it deserves a mention for its huge tithe barn and its once fortified manor house, Ashleworth Court, both of which, along with the church, are close to the water. The rest of the village is built well away from possible floods.

BERKELEY

Gloucestershire is short on castles. There are only two of note, Sudeley and Berkeley; and while Sudeley epitomise Renaissance England, Berkeley seems to belong to the more bellicose Middle Ages. It is altogether a more fortress-like concoction of towers and dense walls, in forbidding, purple stone and was the home of one of the region's most powerful families, whose descendants have lived here for more than 800 years.

The castle domain was granted to the Fitzharding family in 1153 by Henry II from which period most of the current building dates. Following his deposition, Edward II was murdered here in 1327 in the King's Gallery. There is much to enjoy – the dungeons, the Great Hall, the Morning Room with its magnificent medieval ceiling, and a wonderful collection of works of art, including silverware, furniture and tapestries. In the western wall is the huge breach made by the Parliamentary army during the Civil War.

Close by is the Church of St Mary, in Early English style. If it is open you will find some interesting items. Among the wall decorations is a Doom painting (to urge people away from the path of sin) above the chancel arch, while the Berkeley tombs are just off the chancel.

A short distance from the castle, the Jenner Museum is dedicated to the life and work of a local man, Edward Jenner (1749–1823), who discovered the secret of vaccination against smallpox. The museum is in the handsome Georgian house where he lived. Jenner is buried in the chancel of the church.

BERKELEY CASTLE

CHELTENHAM

Built against the base of the Cotswold escarpment, overlooked by Cleeve and Leckhampton Hills, Cheltenham is ideal for visiting the Cotswolds, the Severn Vale, the Forest of Dean and the Wye Valley. It also plays host to several festivals: a Folk Festival in February; the National Hunt Festival when the Gold Cup is run; Jazz in April; the Science Festival in June; the Summer Cricket Festival and the Music Festival in July; and the Literature Festival in October.

Cheltenham is associated with the Regency period, when a market town of comparative insignificance became a fashionable watering hole. The ensuing building boom has left a town of considerable elegance, of handsome, wide streets lined with Regency-style villas and terraces.

The centre is fairly compact and can easily be explored on foot. The original town ran along the current High Street, now home to major chain stores and two shopping arcades. The Regency town spread southwards along the Promenade, one of the finest thoroughfares in the country, today lined with elegant shops. The terrace at the northern end, built to house those coming to take the waters, now houses the Municipal Offices and the Tourist Information Centre. In front is the Neptune Fountain and a statue to Edward Wilson, the Cheltenham botanist who accompanied Captain Scott on his ill-fated expedition to the South Pole.

Visit

DECORATIVE IRONWORK

Cheltenham is noted for its ironwork which decorates many of the early buildings of the town. Distinctive balconies of finely wrought iron adorn many of the elegant buildings, adding a continental atmosphere to the streets and squares. Particularly fine examples are to be found along Oxford Parade, Royal Parade and Suffolk Square.

The Promenade continues gently up, passing the Imperial Garden and the Town Hall on the left, and reaching the imposing, porticoed façade of the Queens Hotel, built on the site of the Imperial Well. The Imperial Well was one of several that were developed to cash in on the spa boom, but by 1837 the owners decided to concentrate on the Montpellier Spa, also theirs, and build a hotel instead.

The road narrows between the shops here. It is worth walking along Queens Circus towards Fauconberg Street, on the right, a short way – on the right is Cheltenham Ladies' College, part of which conceals the original Royal Well; on the left is one of Cheltenham's loveliest streets, Montpellier Street, which is lined with interesting shops raised from the road behind wide pavements. A small alleyway on the left from Montpellier Street leads back towards the main road passing old Montpellier Arcade to the left. At the top of the road is the Rotunda,

now a bank although originally the Montpellier Spa, its design was apparently based on the Pantheon in Rome. The well-preserved interior is worth a look.

If you have the time there is a good deal more Regency architecture to enjoy in the area close to Montpellier, notably in Lansdowne, which is just to the west of Montpellier. Heading southeast will take you to Suffolk Square, just beyond which, along Suffolk Parade and Suffolk Road, are some interesting antique and curio shops.

North of the High Street is Pittville and its showpiece, the Pittville Pump Rooms. The Pump Rooms constitute a magnificent architectural ensemble and were designed between 1825 and 1830 by a local man, John Forbes. They were to be the focal point of Joseph Pitt's Pittville Estate. His legacies are the Pump Rooms, Pittville Park with its lake surrounded by villas in an array of fantastic styles, Pittville Lawn, Clarence Square and Wellington

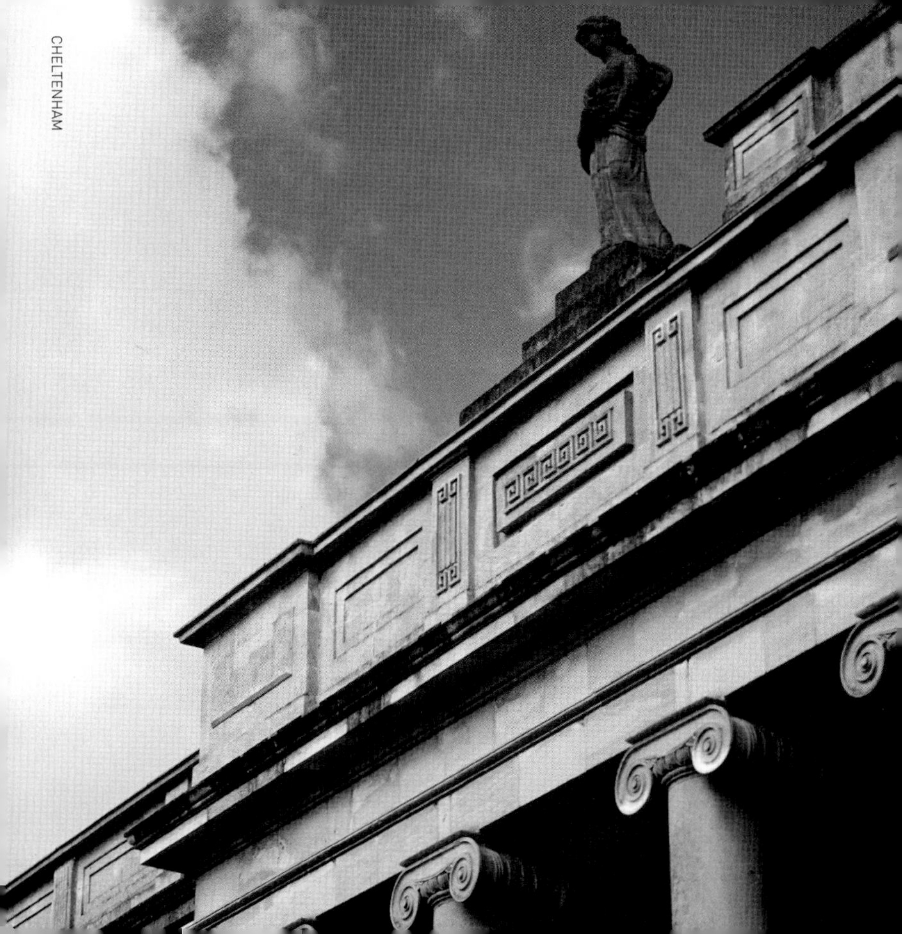

Square. In the Pump Rooms, which are often used for concerts and recitals, you can taste the waters or visit the museum on the upper floor.

The city art gallery and museum, on Clarence Street, deserves a visit. While the collection is an eclectic one, there are several areas of specialisation, notably the work of the 19th-century Arts and Crafts Movement, an impressive display of oriental porcelain, and an exhibition devoted to the life of the Antarctic explorer, Edward Wilson.

Cheltenham's most famous son is the composer Gustav Holst, who was born here in 1874. The house where he grew up in Clarence Road is now a museum dedicated, in part, to the life of the composer and partly to an evocation of life in the Regency and Victorian city. Holst was a pupil at the local grammar school and by the age of 17 he had already heard his marvellous *scherzo* performed at Montpellier Rotunda.

There are a number of villages in the vicinity of Cheltenham worth

Visit

CHELTENHAM RACECOURSE

A visit to the racecourse is a 'must' for anyone interested in watching the world's best chasers and hurdlers. The track is best known for the National Hunt Festival in March, the top three-day meeting of the season which features the Gold Cup and Champion Hurdle and attracts more than 50,000 spectators. The Hall of Fame tells the story of the history of the racecourse.

visiting. Many are mentioned under their own heading but, among those that are not, Prestbury, home of the racecourse, must not be overlooked as it claims to be the most haunted village in Britain. Syde and Brimpsfield, 5 miles (8km) to the south of Cheltenham, are noted for their interesting churches; and Miserden, an estate village of some charm is close to Misarden Park, an Elizabethan mansion set in glorious gardens which are open to the public and worth a visit.

Insight

SEVERN BORE

The Severn Bore, the wave that travels along the lower reaches of the river, can be up to 9 feet (just under 3m) high. It is caused by the tidal movements of the Bristol Channel and the Severn Estuary, which experiences one of the greatest tidal ranges in the world. At low tide the water recedes exposing an extensive area of mudflats, which are rapidly covered by the returning tide. The local press reports on its movements and two of the best vantage points are Stonebench and Minsterworth.

DEERHURST & ODDA'S CHAPEL

An attractive vale farming village, with some fine examples of cruck-construction timber-framed houses, Deerhurst is located on the wide, grassy east bank of the Severn. Its claims to fame are a Saxon parish church and chapel.

St Mary's Priory, was once part of an important 8th-century monastery. The church is the only remaining Saxon monastic church in the country and has several Saxon doors and windows and a 9th-century font (the finest in England). Particularly striking is the double-headed window high up on the west wall, which is possibly made up of Roman stones; the animal-headed label stops (the carved ends of dripstones) in the middle doorway below date from the early 9th century. The Deerhurst Angel is the name of a carving, also from the 9th century, on the surviving arch of the Saxon apse, now on the east exterior.

A mere 200 yards (183m) southwest of the church is a stone building seemingly tacked onto a half-timbered Tudor farmhouse. This is Odda's Chapel, once concealed behind walls added throughout later centuries and only revealed as a complete Saxon chapel in 1885. The discovery of an inscribed tablet, the Odda Stone, dates its construction to 1056. When discovered the chancel had been divided with floors, while the nave had become a kitchen.

GLOUCESTER CATHEDRAL

GLOUCESTER

For a town of such immense historical importance, Gloucester has suffered aesthetically. There is, in fact, quite a lot to see, but with the obvious exception of the cathedral, it has to be sought out. For many centuries, Gloucester was one of the most important cities in the kingdom. It was founded as Roman *Glevum*, at first as a garrison town on the western edge of occupied England and then as a *colonia*, populated by retired legionnaires, who were rewarded with a villa and a sinecure. Under the Saxons it regained importance in the 7th century when the monastery of St Peter was established; the modern street plan is closer to the Saxon rather than the Roman town. Once it had become the capital of a Saxon shire, Edward the Confessor held his winter court here, a tradition continued by William I, who announced in Gloucester his great undertaking, the Domesday Book. Soon after, work started on the abbey church that was to become the city's landmark, its Cathedral of St Peter. In 1216 Henry III was crowned in Gloucester (the only monarch to have been crowned outside Westminster) and in 1327 the murdered Edward II was buried here, a fact that subsequently turned Gloucester into a place of pilgrimage until the Dissolution of the Monasteries.

The points of interest are scattered throughout the city and an early visit to the Tourist Information Centre in St Michael's Tower at The Cross is a good idea. This is the site of the 13th-century stone cross removed in 1751 'for the better conveniency of carriages', and is the meeting point of the city's four principal streets – Westgate, Eastgate, Southgate and Northgate.

Gloucester Cathedral is just to the north of The Cross, its monumental tower visible from afar. Built on the site of a Saxon abbey, it was William I who appointed Serlo, a Benedictine monk from Mont St

GLOUCESTER CATHEDRAL

GLOUCESTER

Michel, as abbot. Serlo resuscitated the ailing abbey and began its reconstruction during the reign of William Rufus. It was consecrated in 1100 and completed in 1120, although additions were made over the following centuries. At the Dissolution of the Monasteries, the Abbey Church of St Peter was rededicated to the Holy and Invisible Trinity, becoming the cathedral church of the new diocese of Gloucester. It is an outstanding example of medieval ecclesiastical architecture, a successful blend of Norman and Perpendicular.

The tower, dating from 1450, replaces the earlier smaller tower and spire and contains Great Peter, the last medieval Bourdon bell. The nave is lined with magnificent Norman arcading, its vault dating back to 1242 together with the roof which was constructed from 110 oak trees from the Forest of Dean. The South Transept is a very early example of the Perpendicular style, while the Norman crypt reflects the original Norman church above. See, too, the massive east window of 1349 and the beautifully carved 14th-century choirstalls,. Also, the Lady Chapel in late-Perpendicular style, the tomb of Edward II and the Norman chapter house. The beautiful cloisters feature in two of the Harry Potter films.

The Cathedral Green is surrounded by houses from the 16th, 17th and 18th centuries, as well as the 15th-century half-timbered Parliament Room, where Richard II held Parliament in 1378.

The docks themselves have long since been redundant but the area has been restored and is worth a walk around. Warehouses have been resurrected as offices, restaurants and museums, among them the National Waterways Museum. In another warehouse is the Gloucester Antiques Centre with 60 shops to browse. At the north end of the docks the Old Custom House is home to the Soldiers of Gloucestershire Museum.

Activity

GLOUCESTER & SHARPNESS CANAL

Originally it was hoped to build a canal from Berkeley Pill to Gloucester to avoid the difficult Severn route but it was only in 1827 that a shorter version from Sharpness, where the Old Dock was linked by a lock to the Severn, saw the light of day. The New Dock, still used, was built in 1874. Near by is a large stone pier, all that remains of the 1879 Severn Railway Bridge which was demolished in 1969 after being struck by a ship. The canal banks are dotted with a number of charming bridge-keepers' cottages decorated with Doric columns. If you have the energy, you can walk the whole 16-mile (25.7km) length of the canal along the towpath.

A walk through the bustle of the city's main streets is recommended. The medieval New Inn, a short way from The Cross along Northgate Street, designed to accommodate the growing number of visitors to the tomb of Edward II in the 15th century, is built around a beautiful galleried courtyard. On Southgate Street, the Church of St Mary de Crypt is a fine example of the Perpendicular style, although in its history its crypt has been a tavern and the whole church became an explosives factory during the Siege of Gloucester in 1643.

Some remains of the Roman Wall can be viewed under the City Museum, while Blackfriars is the finest surviving Dominican Friary in the country, and is undergoing restoration. For aficionados of museums there are several others worth seeing – Gloucester City Museum and Art Gallery on Brunswick Road contains Roman mosaics and the Birdlip Mirror, together with a Natural History section with a freshwater aquarium, and an excellent art collection. The Folk Museum is housed in some fine half-timbered houses on Westgate Street. Not far from here is Ladybellgate House, the finest town house in Gloucester.

NATIONAL WATERWAYS MUSEUM
LLANTHONY WAREHOUSE

LLANTHONY WAREHOUSE
NATIONAL WATERWAYS MUSEUM

GLOUCESTER DOCKS

Just a few miles to the south of Gloucester on a Cotswold outlier, standing 651 feet (198m) high, is the Robinswood Hill Country Park, where there is a rare breeds farm. The old quarry on its west side is a Site of Special Scientific Interest because of its exposure of lower and middle lias rock, the finest inland example in the country.

SLIMBRIDGE

The Wildfowl and Wetlands Trust at Slimbridge is the inspiration of the late Sir Peter Scott, artist and naturalist. Established as the Severn Wildfowl Trust in 1946, the saltmarshes around the Gloucester and Sharpness Canal and the River Severn have now become the home of the greatest collection of waterfowl in the world, from swans to flamingos. Excellent viewing facilities are available and, in winter, towers and hides provide remarkable views of migrating birds. There are also displays of wildlife art and many other attractions.

Visit

WINTER VISITORS

Slimbridge is the winter home of Bewick's swans, which migrate every year from Siberia, and whooper swans, which come mainly from Iceland. They pair for life and some pairs have been coming to Slimbridge for more than 25 years. The Trust operates an adoption scheme to help ensure their future.

The village itself is certainly well worth a visit and boasts a superb 13th-century church, a very fine example of Early English style. Behind the church is the Rectory, which stands on the site of the early Manor House from where Maurice of Berkeley, a scion of the great Berkeley dynasty, left to fight at the Battle of Bannockburn in 1314. Slimbridge is a possible birthplace of William Tyndale, translator of the Bible into English, but so is North Nibley where there is a monument to the great man.

Two miles (3.2km) north of Slimbridge is Frampton-on-Severn, an extensive village which is said to have the longest village green (22 acres/9ha) in England. The restored church contains a rare lead Norman font, which is worthy of inspection.

TEWKESBURY

Tewkesbury's considerable historical significance was largely governed by its location on the banks of the rivers Severn and Avon which were instrumental in the 16th-century cloth and mustard trade and later the flour trade. Its importance depended, too, on its medieval Benedictine monastery of which only the magnificent church remains. The monastery was built by the Norman, Robert Fitzhamon, who used the Severn to import stone from Normandy for its construction. After his death the 'Honour of Tewkesbury', as the patronage came to be known, passed to an illegitimate son of Henry I and then to the de Clare family.

The abbey became one of the most powerful in the kingdom, owning large areas of sheep grazing land and building many fine tithe barns in the process – some of these survive, for example at Stanway. The abbey was dissolved in 1539 but Tewkesbury's citizens bought the church for the total sum of £483.

However, due to its unfortunate location close to two rivers which, even now, tend to flood, and with the abbey lands at its back, the town, unable to expand, folded in on itself.

Throughout the 17th and 18th centuries this was achieved by building around narrow alleyways, several of which have survived (Machine Court, Fish Alley, Fryzier Alley) off the main streets – Barton Street, Church Street and High Street. There is, therefore, a great deal more of Tewkesbury than is at first evident to the eye, although its marvellous collection of half-timbered and brick houses presents one of the finest historical ensembles in the country.

TEWKESBURY

However, the town is dominated by the Abbey Church of St Mary and the eye filled by its great 148-foot (45m) square Norman tower. Inside, one of the most striking features is the 14 Norman pillars supporting the 14th-century roof. The choir is illuminated by 14th-century stained-glass windows, while around it radiate six chapels containing various monuments to the wealthy families that have influenced both the church and the town. The west front exterior is notable for its dramatic Norman arch, of almost unsurpassed grandeur.

A circular town walk includes, in dry weather, a stroll across the Ham – an enormous meadow that separates the Mill Avon from the Severn and which invariably floods each winter – to the river.

Opposite the church is the handsome Bell Hotel. From here Mill Street leads you down to Abel Fletcher's Mill (Abbey Mill), so called because it is thought to have played a role in the Victorian novel,

Visit

ANCIENT INNS

Tewkesbury has a number of old and interesting inns. The Royal Hop Pole in Church Street was featured in *The Pickwick Papers*, the novel by Charles Dickens; the Tudor House in the High Street was built in 1540 by the Pilgrim Fathers, Ye Olde Black Bear near the junction with Mythe Road and High Street possibly dates back to 1308, while the Ancient Grudge takes its name from the Wars of the Roses.

John Halifax, Gentleman, much of which is set in the fictional town of Nortonbury, which was modelled on Tewkesbury. From here you can either walk along St Mary's Road, with its attractive timbered cottages, or cross the Avon and strike out across the Severn Ham. Every year the grass of the Ham, which is owned by the town, is cut and auctioned off according to a centuries-old tradition.

Insight

LITERARY ASSOCIATIONS

Tewkesbury has several literary associations as we have seen. There are others; Barbara Cartland (1901–2000) had links with the town and the family monument is to be found in the churchyard. The organ within the abbey church was played by the poet John Milton when it was located at Hampton Court. Daniel Defoe's observations on the town are recorded in his *Tour through the Whole Island of Great Britain*, (published 1724–26). He called Tewkesbury 'a large and very populous town situated upon the River Avon' famous 'for a great manufacture of stockings'. Seventy years later the essayist William Hazlitt, walking from Shropshire to Somerset, recorded how he spent a night in a Tewkesbury inn reading Saint Pierre's *Paul and Virginia*.

At the Severn turn right to walk along by the weir and then return across the meadow this side of the flour mills. You can cross the old mill bridge and then walk along the Avon. At King John's Bridge recross the river and turn right into the High Street to the The Cross, now a memorial but the site of the medieval High Cross that was razed by Puritans in 1650.

On your left Barton Street will take you to the fascinating Tewkesbury Museum, located in a 17th-century building that also houses the Tourist Information Centre. The museum features a model of the Battle of Tewkesbury. Church Street, to your right, takes you past the distinctive Royal Hop Pole Hotel, which featured famously in Charles Dickens' novel *The Pickwick Papers*. Beyond this is a row of restored 15th-century cottages built by medieval merchants. One, known as the Merchant's House, is presented as it would have looked in its heyday. Another, the John

TEWKESBURY

Moore Countryside Museum, takes its name from the local writer whose stories were based on Tewkesbury and the countryside and villages around nearby Bredon.

On the right, an alleyway leads down to the Old Baptist Chapel and Court. Although the building dates back to the 15th century, it became a chapel only in the 17th century.

THORNBURY

An attractive market town just north of Bristol in the county of Gloucestershire, Thornbury is well known for its Tudor castle, built in 1510 by Edward Stafford, 3rd Duke of Buckingham, Constable of England. After the Duke was executed on charges of treason, Thornbury Castle was appropriated by Henry VIII and he stayed here with Anne Boleyn in 1535. Mary Tudor returned the castle to the Staffords but after the Civil War it fell to ruin until 1824 when it became the residence of the Howard family. Now a luxury hotel, it is particularly noted for the handsome

Activity

'BLOODY MEADOW'

After the Battle of Tewkesbury in 1417, perhaps the most decisive battle of the Wars of the Roses, many of the defeated Lancastrian troops sought sanctuary in the church but were slain nonetheless. 'Bloody Meadow' as the battlefield came to be known, is south of the church, off Lincoln Green Lane, and there is a 'Battlefield Trail' to follow.

brick double chimney and the fine tracery of its oriel windows.

The Church of St Mary the Virgin has a fine medieval tower which apparently sways a full 6 inches (15cm) when the peal of eight bells is rung. Inside there is an unusual medieval stone pulpit. A cottage on Chapel Street now houses Thornbury Museum, with its exhibits on local life and heritage. The museum also hosts special events and can organise guided walks and tours.

TOURIST INFORMATION OFFICES

Cheltenham
Cheltenham Municipal Offices,
77 The Promenade.
Tel: 01242 522878;
www.visitcheltenham.gov.uk

Gloucester
28 Southgate Street.
Tel: 01452 421188
National Waterways Museum.
Tel: 01452 318061

Tewkesbury
The Museum, 64 Barton Street.
Tel: 01684 295027;
www.tewkesburybc.gov.uk

Thornbury
The Town Hall, Old Police Station,
High Street.
Tel: 01454 281638

PLACES OF INTEREST

Ashleworth Tithe Barn
Tel: 01452 814213;
www.nationaltrust.org.uk

Berkeley Castle
Tel: 01453 810332;
www.berkeley-castle.com
Also butterfly house.

Blackfriars Dominican Friary
Ladybellgate, Gloucester.
Tel: 0117 9750700;
www.english-heritage.org

Cheltenham Art Gallery and Museum
Clarence Street, Cheltenham.
Tel: 01242 237431;
www.cheltenhammuseum.org.uk

Cheltenham Racecourse Hall of Fame
The Racecourse, Prestbury Park,
Cheltenham. Tel: 01242 513014.

City Museum and Art Gallery
Brunswick Road, Gloucester.
Tel: 01452 396131;
www.glos-city.gov.uk

Gloucester Cathedral
College Green, Gloucester.
Tel: 01452 508095;
www.gloucestercathedral.org.uk

Gloucester Docks
The Docks, Gloucester.
Tel: 01452 311190;
www.gloucesterdocks.me.uk

Gloucester Folk Museum
99–103 Westgate Street, Gloucester.
Tel: 01452 396868;
www.gloucester.gov.uk

Holst Birthplace Museum
4 Clarence Road, Pittville, Cheltenham.
Tel: 01242 524846;
www.holstmuseum.org.uk

Jenner Museum
Church Lane, Berkeley.
Tel: 01453 810631;
www.jennermuseum.com

John Moore Countryside Museum
41 Church Street, Tewkesbury.
Tel: 01684 297174;
www.gloster.demon.co.uk

Merchant's House
45 Church Street, Tewkesbury.
Tel: 01684 297174

Misarden Park Gardens
Miserden.
Tel: 01285 821303

National Waterways Museum
Llanthony Warehouse, Gloucester
Docks, Gloucester.
Tel: 01452 318200;
www.nwm.org.uk

Nature in Art
Wallsworth Hall, Tewkesbury Road,
Twigworth, Gloucester.
Tel: 01452 731422;
www.nature-in-art.org.uk

Odda's Chapel
Off B4213, Deerhurst.
www.englishheritage.org.uk/visits

Oldbury Power Station
Oldbury.
Tel: 01454 419899

Pittville Pump Room and Museum
Pittville Park, Cheltenham.
Tel: 01242 523852.

Soldiers of Gloucestershire Museum
Custom House, The Docks, Gloucester.
Tel: 01452 522682;
www.glosters.org.uk

Tewkesbury Abbey
Church Street, Tewkesbury.
Tel: 01684 850959;
www.tewkesburyabbey.org.uk

Tewkesbury Town Museum
64 Barton Street, Tewkesbury.
Tel: 01684 292901;
www.tewkesburymuseum.org.uk

Wildfowl and Wetlands Trust
Slimbridge.
Tel: 01453 890333;
www.wwt.org.uk/visit/slimbridge

SEVERN VALE

FOR CHILDREN
St Augustine's Farm
Arlingham, Gloucester.
Tel: 01452 740277
Rare Breeds Farm
Robinswood Hill Country Park,
Gloucester.
Tel: 01452 303206

SHOPPING
Cheltenham
Farmers' Market on the Promenade on
the second and last Friday each month.
For antiques and crafts shops: Suffolk
Road, Suffolk Parade.
Gloucester
Market, Wed.
The Made in Gloucestershire Shop,
23 Westgate Street. Tel: 07813 943237
Tewkesbury
Farmers' Market, Wed.
Market, Sat.

PERFORMING ARTS
Everyman Theatre
Regent Street, Cheltenham.
Tel: 01242 572573;
www.everymantheatre.org.uk

Guildhall Arts Centre
23 Eastgate Street, Gloucester.
Tel: 01452 396370;
www.gloucester.gov.uk
Kings Theatre
Kingsbarton Street, Gloucester.
Tel: 01452 300130;
www.kingstheatre.uk2k.com
New Olympus Theatre
Barton Street, Gloucester.
Tel: 01452 525917;
www.newolympustheatre.co.uk
Playhouse Theatre
47–53 Bath Road, Cheltenham.
Tel: 01242 522852;
www.playhousecheltenham.org
Roses Theatre
Sun Street, Tewkesbury.
Tel: 01684 295074;
www.rosestheatre.org
Sub Tone
117 Promenade, Cheltenham.
Tel: 01242 575925

SPORTS & ACTIVITIES
BOAT HIRE
Tewkesbury
Telstar Cruisers.
Tel: 01684 294088
BOAT TRIPS
River Severn Cruises operate from
Upton-on-Severn.
Tel: 01684 593112
CYCLING
Cheltenham
Compass Holidays,
48 Shurdington Road.
Tel: 01242 250642
GUIDED WALKS
Cotswolds Walking Holidays,
30 Imperial Square, Cheltenham.
Tel: 01242 254353;
www.cotswoldwalks.com.
The Voluntary Wardens arrange
guided walks.
Tel: 01451 862000;
www.cotswoldsaonb.org.uk
HORSE RACING
Cheltenham
Cheltenham Racecourse, Prestbury
Park, Cheltenham.
Tel: 01242 513014

HORSE-RIDING
Brookthorpe
Cotswold Trail Riding, Ongers Farm,
Upton Lane.
Tel: 01452 813344
Hardwicke
Summer House Education and
Equitation Centre.
Tel: 01452 720288
SKIING
Gloucester Ski and Snowboard Centre
Robinswood Hill Dry Ski Slope.
Tel: 08702 400375

ANNUAL EVENTS & CUSTOMS
Cheltenham
Folk Festival, Feb.
National Hunt, Prestbury Park, Mar.
Jazz Festival, Apr/May.
Science Festival, Jun.
International Festival of Music, Jul.
Gloucester
Gloucester Cricket Festival, May.
Three Choirs Festival, held either in
Gloucester, Hereford or Worcester.
Tewkesbury
Food Festival, May.
Medieval Fair, Jul.

121

TEA ROOMS

Druckers

28–29 Regent Arcade,
Cheltenham, GL50 1JZ
Tel: 01242 524440
www.druckers.co.uk

One of a chain founded in Birmingham by Austrian Andre Drucker in 1964, this is an opportunity to enjoy authentic Viennese cakes and pastries in a smart, modern setting.

Thatchers Tea Rooms

101 Montpellier Street, Cheltenham
Tel: 01242 584150

An elegant Georgian building houses this welcoming tea room is an ideal place to rest after the rigours of shopping. Enjoy the calm and relaxing atmosphere while sampling a traditional English afternoon tea.

The Coffee Shop

Gloucester Cathedral,
Gloucester, GL1 2LR
Tel: 01452 733945
www.gloucestercathedral.org.uk

Situated just off the famous cloisters, this friendly place serves teas, coffee, delicious soup, scones and irresistible cakes. Scenes in the early Harry Potter films were shot in these cloisters.

Haywards Coffee Shop

Nature in Art, Wallsworth Hall,
Twigworth, GL2 9PA
Tel: 01452 731422

A light and airy conservatory houses the coffee shop at the Nature in Art collection, (admission to the coffee shop is free), where a tempting range of cream teas and cakes that are all baked on the premises is available.

Boat Inn

The Quay, Ashleworth, GL19 4HZ
Tel: 01452 700272
www.boat-inn.co.uk

A gem of a pub set beside the river, with a tiny front parlour, but plenty of seating outside to enjoy the view. Local beers accompany generously filled rolls or a ploughman's lunch.

The Malt House

Marybrook Street, Berkeley, GL13 9BA
Tel: 01453 511177
www.themalthouse.uk.com

Close to Berkeley Castle, this is a family run pub/restaurant with rooms. The dining room is large and comfortable, and a good selection of meat, fish and vegetarian dishes is always available.

The Farmers Arms

Ledbury Road, Lower Apperley, GL19 4DR
Tel: 01452 780307

This is a popular country pub with low beams and a menu to suit most tastes. Fresh fish is the house speciality.

The Anchor Inn

Church Road, Oldbury-on-Severn, BS35 1QA
Tel: 01454 413331

Originally a mill house, parts of this stone pub date back to 1540. Plenty of traditional English dishes are served in a friendly atmosphere, while outside a pretty stream flows by the large garden and this is a lovely spot to enjoy a meal.

The Fleet Inn

Twyning, Nr Tewkesbury, GL20 6FL
Tel: 01684 274310
www.fleet-inn.co.uk

With a wonderful setting on the banks of the River Avon, this popular pub offers a range of food from light snacks, to a carvery and full three-course meals. The inside has a cosy atmosphere, complete with an inglenook fireplace and there is a large patio outside. Keg bitters and draft cider are available at the bar.

COTSWOLD WATER PARK

Southern Cotswolds

BATH

BADMINTON

BIBURY

CASTLE COMBE

CHEDWORTH

CIRENCESTER

THE COLN VALLEY

THE DUNTISBOURNES

DURSLEY

DYRHAM

MINCHINHAMPTON

NORTHLEACH

PAINSWICK

PRINKNASH

THE SODBURYS

SOUTH CERNEY & THE
COTSWOLD WATER PARK

STROUD VALLEY

TETBURY

ULEY & OWLPEN

WOTTON-UNDER-EDGE

INTRODUCTION

The southern Cotswolds
are different in character
from the northern part – the
escarpment is lower, but
the valleys are steeper; and
the dappled stone is heavier
seeming, in keeping with the
area's industrial heritage.
The medieval wool industry
moved from the high wolds
to these steeper valleys to
make use of the fast-flowing
streams, above all in the
Stroud Valley. Pretty villages
abound, particularly along the
Coln Valley while the Roman
Cotswolds are embodied
in marvellous towns and
villages, such as Cirencester,
Chedworth and Bath.

Unmissable attractions

Enjoy beautiful architecture, great shopping and a choice of stylish places to eat at Bath...be enthralled by the mosaics at Chedworth Roman Villa or the famous spa at Bath...admire 17th-century Arlington Row's of cottages at Bibury filled with traditional chocolate-box charm...have watery fun at the Cotswold Water Park and South Cerney – waterskiing, windsurfing and kayaking plus birdwatching, angling and cycling...enjoy year-round colour at Westonbirt Arboretum...explore Cirencester and don't miss the geometric landscaping at Cirencester Park...explore 'The Queen of the Cotswolds', Painswick, and admire the houses built by wealthy wool merchants.

1

1 Chedworth Roman Villa

Much of the mosaic work at Chedworth Roman Villa is thought to have been produced at Cirencester, where craftsmen had developed their own style, known as the Corinium school.

2 Arlington Row, Bibury

These 17th-century cottages were built as homes for the weavers who worked for the mill in the village. The homes were effectively workshops as the weavers worked in them for piece rates.

131

3 Canal at Lechlade

The highest navigable stretch of the Thames attracts pleasure craft and canal boats, especially in the summer months.

4 St Mary's Church, Painswick

The churchyard is notable for its 99 yew trees. The trees have become heavily entwined making it difficult to count them.

4

BATH

One of the finest towns in Europe, Bath is known chiefly for its Roman baths and for the elegance of its Georgian architecture, the result of its fashionable re-emergence as a spa in the 18th century. Although not a Cotswold town, Bath is nonetheless inseparable from the area, not least because its buildings are made of Cotswold limestone.

Archaeological evidence indicates that the first settlement here, *Aquae Sulis*, was Roman. Later, an important Saxon abbey was built, and later a Norman cathedral. The famous waters continued to 'taken', but it wasn't until the 17th century that the fashion for medicinal waters led to new building under the sponsorship of Master of Ceremonies, Richard 'Beau' Nash, architect John Wood and, later, City Surveyor, Thomas Baldwin.

The town is dramatically situated over the surrounding hills, presenting a magnificent aspect. There is a great deal to see in Bath but many of the highlights can be enjoyed on foot. Since parking can be a problem, use the park-and-ride system. The bus from the Lansdown car park sets you down at Queen's Square, which is a good place to start your tour of the city.

The centre of Bath can be divided into four – the oldest part is the city centre around the abbey and baths; the Upper Town was built as the town expanded, while Kingsmead is the liveliest area at night. Bathwick and Widcombe are west of the Pulteney Bridge. The following walk takes in part of the first three areas; places not featured are described afterwards.

Queen Square was John Wood's first important work and takes its name from Queen Caroline, consort of George II. The obelisk in the centre was built to honour the visit of the Prince and Princess of Wales in 1738. Wood's masterpiece, the Circus, begun in 1754, is at the top of Gay Street, which runs north along the east side of Queen Square and

Visit

THERMAE BATH SPA

The Thermae Bath Spa provides the city with the only working traditional spa in the United Kingdom. The historic Cross Bath and the Hot (or Old Royal) Bath have undergone major work to restore the original use of these Grade 1 buidings. The Cross Bath has been officially recognised as a sacred site. There is also a restaurant and a visitor centre.

passes the Jane Austen Centre on the right. The Circus is a design of great originality, the façade of each of the three floors is framed in a series of columns, from bottom to top, Doric, Ionic and Corinthian.

From here it is a stroll west along Brock Street to another marvellous ensemble, the Royal Crescent, begun by John Wood's son in 1767. Number 1, open to the public, has been restored to look as it would have done 200 years ago. A longer walk takes you further north to other crescents, those of Camden, Cavendish, Lansdown and Somerset Place. Behind Lansdown Crescent is Beckford's Walk, replete with the follies placed there by the eccentric millionaire William Beckford.

Gravel Walk, opposite No 1 Royal Crescent, threads through parkland and shortly turns left, past the Georgian Garden, to Queen's Parade Place. Turn left, then left again to re-enter Gay Street and then turn right into George Street and right again into Milsom Street. Continue into Burton Street as it becomes Union Street and turn left into Northumberland Place. Pass through this little alley of shops to the High Street and cross over to the Guildhall. Designed in 1776 by Thomas Baldwin this has a sumptuous Adam-style banqueting room with elegant 18th-century crystal chandeliers.

Beyond the Guildhall is the covered market. On the far side of the market is Grand Parade and the River Avon and to the left the

ROMAN BATHS

BATH

magnificence of Pulteney Bridge, designed by Robert Adam in 1769 and one of only a few bridges in the world lined by shops on both sides. On the other side of the bridge is a marvellous vista down Great Pulteney Street towards the Holburne Museum and steps down to the riverside walk.

Turning right along Grand Parade will bring you to Orange Grove. Pass the east end of the abbey and continue down Terrace Walk. By the Huntsman Inn, turn right down North Parade Passage to Sally Lunn's House, built in 1622 and one of the oldest houses in Bath. Here Sally Lunn created her famous Bath buns and the original faggot oven and period kitchenware are still exhibited. Although it is still a coffee house, it is also a museum and the medieval and Roman excavations are the largest on show in Bath.

North Parade Passage emerges at Abbey Green. Turn right here for the abbey itself, the third to be built on this site. The first was built in the 8th century by Offa, King of Mercia. The 12th-century Norman abbey fell into disrepair and was replaced by this smaller version. Inside, after passing a manned desk where 'voluntary' payment is expected, there is much to admire – its magnificent ceiling and windows, and array of plaques, some of which make fascinating reading. The Heritage Vaults tell the abbey's story and include Saxon and Norman stonework and a reconstruction of the Norman cathedral.

In the courtyard, a favourite place with buskers and other performers, the National Trust shop is in Marshall Wade's House, the oldest Palladian style building in Bath. Opposite are the Roman baths, the best-preserved Roman religious spa from the ancient world. The remains of a temple can be seen here, as well as objects discovered in the area of the baths over the centuries. Next door are the elegant Pump Rooms, a great venue for coffee, lunch or even a glass of the

Activity

CYCLE ROUTE

Bath has a cycle route, the Avon Cycleway, which follows the disused railway line through the city along the course of the Avon river valley. The complete cycleway is an 85-mile (137km) circular route, taking in Bristol, Thornbury and picturesque villages. You can get maps of the route from the Tourist Information Centre.

fairly unpleasant-tasting mineral water. Any of these things can be taken accompanied by period music played by the Pump Rooms Trio.

From Abbey Church Yard turn left into Stall Street, then right along Bath Street to Cross Bath, a delightful example of Bath's former hot mineral water sources, housed in an 18th-century building and with the Thermae Bath Spa to the left. Beyond, on the right of Cross Bath, is the entrance to St John's Hospital, a medieval foundation, still offering sheltered housing.

Take the wide pavement further to the right of Cross Bath, turning left by Chandos Buildings, and continue past the back of the Hospital to the road, Westgate Buildings. Turn right until you reach Sawclose to the right. Before continuing up there have a look at Kingsmead Square on the left, where Rosewell House is a rare example of the baroque style in the city.

Continue up Sawclose where the Theatre Royal, opened in 1805, is on the left. Next door is the former home of Beau Nash. Cross the road to enjoy a good view of the theatre and then turn right down Upper Borough Walls.

Along Upper Borough Walls are the surviving remnants of the medieval city wall opposite the Royal National Hospital for Rheumatic Diseases. After the wall turn left down a narrow lane and left again into Trim Street, where General Wolfe's former residence is marked with a memorial plaque. Turn right through Trim Bridge arch to Queen

BATH

Street and left by the junction with Quiet Street into Wood Street, which will bring you back to Queen Square.

There are plenty of other things to see in Bath, including notable and unusual museum collections. In Upper Town the Assembly Rooms, on Bennett Street, were built to complement the Pump Room. In the basement is the Museum of Costume, which covers the history of clothes from the 16th century to the present day. Close by, at Circus Lodge, is the Museum of East Asian Art covering 7,000 years of history to include exhibits of jade, bamboo and lacquer. On the Paragon, in the Countess of Huntingdon's Chapel, is the Building of Bath Museum, which shows how the city was created. Not far from the Assembly Rooms, in Julian Road, is the Museum of Bath at Work, which tells the story of the city's trades and industries.

The Victoria Art Gallery is on Bath Street. It has paintings by British and European Masters, as well as scenes of early Bath. There are also collections of porcelain, watches and other decorative items.

The Holburne Museum of Art, in a Palladian villa, is home to the city's finest collections, particularly silverware, porcelain, furniture and paintings. These treasures are displayed along with examples of 20th-century art and crafts.

Among the interesting places in the area is Beckford's Tower, standing on the summit of Lansdown. It was built in 1825 to house part of William Beckford's art collection and now holds a museum devoted to his life. Two miles (3.2km) southeast of Bath, the American Museum at Claverton Manor, a fine 19th-century house illustrates American life from the 17th to 19th centuries.

BADMINTON

A name that most likely evokes the image of either a feathered shuttlecock and a high net or a three-day equestrian event. The first, the game of badminton was brought from India in the 1870s and takes its name from Badminton House, the demesne of the Dukes of Beaufort; while the second is an annual event of world renown that has taken place on the estate since 1949.

Badminton House (not open), a Palladian house built for the first Duke of Beaufort in 1682, was remodelled by William Kent in 1740. It is considered a particularly fine example of the period style and the interior is wonderfully decorated. The park was partly the work of 'Capability' Brown. Some of the formal layout is on a quite extraordinary scale; the so-called Great Avenue is several miles long and lined with trees.

The 18th-century church of Great Badminton, which is in the estate grounds close to the house, is notable for its monuments to the Beaufort family, one of which, by Grinling Gibbons, is so big that the church had to be altered to accommodate it. The box pews are exceptionally large, like old-fashioned snug bars.

Insight

BEAUFORTSHIRE

The area around Badminton, seat of the Dukes of Beaufort, was known locally as 'Beaufortshire', since it lies in the land of the Beaufort Hunt. There is a print of a chimney sweep at Chipping Sodbury saying 'Sorry, gentlemen, I can't vote for you 'cause I 'unts with the Duke'.

BIBURY

Bibury, one of the most popular of the classic Cotswold villages, was famously described by poet and artist William Morris as the 'most beautiful village in England', a rather risky thing to say, particularly in an area as blessed with handsome villages as the Cotswolds. Still, Bibury is undoubtedly in the first echelon, with the trout-filled Coln river sliding alongside the main street, its exceptionally interesting church and an array of picturesque cottages. Although, strictly speaking, what is considered to be picturesque

is actually in the neighbouring village of Arlington, but the two villages are now indistinguishable.

Bibury was originally a Saxon foundation, although most of what makes Bibury and Arlington (the neighbouring settlement) so attractive dates from around the 17th century when the village prospered as a weaving centre. The church, in a well-tended churchyard at the heart of the original village at the far end of the main street, retains some of its original Saxon work – the chancel arch jambs and the fragments of a cross shaft.

Among the many delightful cottages in the village, those in Arlington Row, a terrace of low-gabled weavers' cottages just across the river towards the church end of the village, are the most famously photogenic. They belong to the National Trust, and are still occupied. Originally they were used by workers weaving wool for Arlington Mill at the other end of the village – they used the Rack Isle in front of the cottages, now a bird sanctuary, for drying wool. The path

Insight

THE BISLEY PIECE

Part of Bibury churchyard is known as the Bisley Piece, the result of a curious story. It seems that at Bisley there was what was called a 'bone hole', where old bones were thrown when old graves were broken into. Some 600 years ago a priest is supposed to have fallen in and died, an incident that apparently angered the Pope himself. Consequently the pontiff forbade burials in Bisley for two years, the residents having, instead, to bury their dead at Bibury, some 15 miles (24km) away.

in front of Arlington Row continues up Awkward Hill lined with attractive cottages, or skirts Rack Isle, parallel to the river, to 17th-century Arlington Mill. This is now open as a museum displaying aspects of local rural life.

Next door is Bibury Trout Farm where you can catch your own fish or make purchases from the shop. Just across the road is the Swan Hotel, once a fashionable haunt for the followers of Bibury Races, which flourished during the 17th century. Now it is an elegant place to stay or to take afternoon tea.

The pretty neighbouring hamlet of Ablington is a collection of cottages, barns and manor houses and the home of the Reverend Arthur Gibbs, the 19th-century author of *A Cotswold Village*.

West of Bibury on the road to Cirencester, is the village of Barnsley. The fine Georgian mansion, Barnsley Park, just outside the village, is not open to the public although there are good walks through the grounds. In the village centre, however, is Rosemary Verey's (1918–2001) Barnsley House Garden, a lovely 18th-century garden featuring herbs, a knot garden and a vegetable garden in the style of a potager. The garden is open only for group tours. Barnsley church has unusual Norman features.

South of Barnsley are the Ampneys, villages set in flat countryside with interesting churches. Down Ampney was the birthplace of the composer Ralph Vaughan Williams, who gave the village name to one of his best known hymns. There is a small exhibition about the composer inside the church.

CASTLE COMBE

Generally considered one of the loveliest villages in the Cotswolds, Castle Combe is very popular and can get crowded. Parking is a problem here and visitors are asked to use the car park. The perfection of this pretty village means that it is also used by film producers.

Like many other Cotswold villages, its wealth came from sheep and wool. Most of the houses here were weavers' houses, and it was allowed to hold a fair for trading sheep and wool. The 14th-century Market Cross, with the old water pump beside it, forms the centre of the village. The nearby Butter Cross was dismantled during the 19th century. The church probably

CASTLE COMBE

dates from the 12th century; one of the interesting items is the clock that used to chime from the tower. A favourite view of the village is from the old weavers' cottages, across the bridge. The museum contains many items of local interest.

Outside the village is the motor racing circuit, which hosted national championship races until the 1990s. Motor sport and other popular events are still held here.

CHEDWORTH

A charming village in itself, the name of Chedworth is usually associated with a Roman villa considered to be the finest in England. Since the two are separated by a mile (1.6km), follow signs to Chedworth or Chedworth Villa, depending on which you want.

Chedworth village, said to be the longest in England, clusters about a lovely old pub. Opposite, a spring pours interminably and a church soars in comparison with the size of the village.

The villa, discovered in 1864, is owned by the National Trust, and is about a mile (1.6km) or a half-hour walk from the village. Although the site looks perfect for a villa, it is thought that the trees that now largely surround it were not there when it was built and that the villa was, instead, in the midst of open farmland. In its time it was one of the largest Roman-British villas in Britain. A short information film about the villa is shown every 15 minutes as part of the entry price.

Most of the original structure of the villa has gone. What remains are the lower parts of the walls, enough to identify the purposes of each of the rooms, and mosaics featuring, among other things, representations of the four seasons. Archaeologists are still hard at work on the site, and there is still a fair amount to be excavated in order to get the full picture. There is a comparatively recent building in the middle, which is the administrator's house that has a small museum attached at its rear.

CIRENCESTER

Now a busy market town, Cirencester was once the most important city in England after London, during the Roman occupation. Called *Corinium Dubunnorum* and founded as a military headquarters in AD 49, a number of important roads radiated from the city – the Fosse Way, Ermin Street and Akeman Street. The Saxons renamed *Corinium* 'Cirencester' (Coryn, meaning 'top part' of the River Churn, the highest source of the Thames; and Ceastre meaning 'fort') but practically destroyed the town, preferring instead to build smaller settlements outside the walls. Only in the Middle Ages did Cirencester regain something of its former glory when it became the most important of the Cotswold wool towns. Markets still take place each Monday and Friday.

The town is most easily explored on foot. There are a number of well signposted car parks within easy reach of the city centre, while the market square is the most convenient place to begin discovery of the town. The 15th-century parish church, one of the largest in England, is the main feature. Its magnificent Perpendicular tower was built with the reward given by Henry IV to a group of local earls who foiled a rebellion. Its fine roof is illuminated by clerestory windows, while the east and west windows are filled with medieval stained glass. The best-known feature of the exterior, however, is the three-storeyed south porch, overlooking the market square, which was built by the abbots in the late 15th century as an office for the abbey (now vanished) and which became the Town Hall after the Dissolution. One of the finest in the country, it was only returned to the church in the 18th century. Inside is a decorative painted wine-goblet style pulpit, several memorial brasses bearing the matrimonial histories of well-known wool merchants and some interesting church plate.

Opposite the church, the Tourist Information Centre is in the Victorian Corn Hall, on the Market Square, which also hosts a weekly market and has a permanent exhibition of local crafts. Cricklade Street, running south from the square, is the site of the Brewery Arts Centre, where craft studios are housed in the old brewery.

On Park Street, close to Cirencester Park, is Corinium Museum, which brings to life many aspects of local history and various finds, including the mosaics that were made in the area from the Roman and later eras. Many are displayed in tableaux form.

Close by is Thomas Street, the location of a 15th-century Weavers Hall almshouse (also known as St Thomas's Hospital) and also Coxwell Street, lined with merchants' houses. Farther north is Spitalgate Lane, with the arcade of the nave of St John's Hospital, and another group of almshouses. Due east from here is the mysterious-looking Spital

Visit

THE KING'S HEAD

On the Market Square in Cirencester is the King's Head, complete with royal keystone over the door. Despite outward appearances the hotel dates back to 1340. In 1642 the Royalist Lord Chandos took refuge in the hotel, thus saving his life, while in 1688 Lord Lovelace, of William of Orange's army, was captured here.

Gate, all that remains of the old abbey. From here a walk through the Abbey Grounds, where the remnants of the Roman walls can be seen at the eastern boundary, will take you back to the town centre.

No visit to Cirencester would be complete without a glimpse, at the very least, of Cirencester Park, probably the finest example of geometric landscaping in the country. It is approached up Cecily Hill, one of the prettiest streets in Cirencester, leading to the wrought iron entrance gates. The park was

Insight

JAMES GIBBS

The Manor House at Winson is a rather unexpected piece of classical architecture in the middle Cotswold vernacular. Its architect was eminent in his field, for James Gibbs designed the Radcliffe Library in Oxford and St Bartholomew's Hospital in London, where the owner of the manor, Surgeon General Howes, was well known.

the conception of the 1st Lord Bathurst in the early 18th century and the house (not open to the public), behind one of the largest yew hedges in the world, was built to his own design. The park was landscaped with the help of the poet Alexander Pope, among others, who has celebrated the construction of the park in verse. In fact there is a corner known as Pope's Seat near the polo ground. It is an excellent place for walking (the grounds are privately owned but open to walkers and riders), especially along the Broad Ride, which stretches from the entrance almost to Sapperton.

Apart from the wall in the Abbey Garden, the only other surviving Roman souvenir is the superb 2nd-century Roman Amphitheatre, which is one of the largest and best preserved in the country. It is found on Cotswold Avenue just south of the Ring Road.

THE COLN VALLEY

The River Coln, a tributary of the Thames, is arguably the loveliest of the many rivers that ripple through the Cotswolds. It rises on the escarpment not far from Cheltenham then gently descends the slopes, passing through a number of pretty villages en route.

Withington has an unusually large church with a fine Norman doorway and a handsome wall monument to Sir John and Lady Howe of Compton Cassey. The 17th-century mansion of Compton Cassey is now a magnificent farmhouse,

lying in splendid isolation in the middle of the valley, forcing the Yanworth road to curve around it. As you approach it you may, for one possibly alarming moment, see a rhinoceros in a field close by. If so it will be the product of the artist's gallery, Compton Cassey Gallery, which now occupies the house.

From here the river passes close to Chedworth Roman Villa and thence to Fossebridge, a steep point on the Roman Fosse Way where an ancient inn continues to attract passing customers. On the other side of the road the Coln furrows across the meadows of Coln St Dennis, a small, silent village built around a modest green, with a small Norman church. Look for the mysterious inscription to Joan Burton on the interior wall of the tower, as well as the Norman corbel stones that now line the nave.

Further on is the pretty hamlet of Calcot and then Coln Rogers with a church remarkable for its Saxon plan and window north of the chancel. At the old mill in Winson, where the road zigzags, there are charming gardens and towards the centre of the village you'll find some converted barns. The compact green is overlooked by a classical looking manor house. After Winson come Ablington and Bibury.

Finally, before going on to Fairford and Lechlade, the Coln arrives at Coln St Aldwyns, where the green is shaded by a magnificent horse chestnut tree and the New Inn is a fine pub. The pretty church has memorial windows commemorating John Keble, the 19th-century reformer, and his father. It is possible to walk along the Coln from here to Bibury.

THE DUNTISBOURNES

A string of villages along the small River Dunt just to the north of Cirencester, the Duntisbournes have a special character on account of their saddleback church towers which have something almost French about them.

Insight

WILLIAM TYNDALE

Southwest of Dursley is Nibley Knoll with its distinctive needle-shaped monolith rising out of the hillside. This is the Tyndale Monument, built in 1886 in honour of William Tyndale, born in nearby North Nibley, and the first man, in 1484, to translate the Bible from Latin into English. It is possible to climb its 111 feet (34m), from where there are excellent views.

Duntisbourne Abbotts was the home of Dr Matthew Baillie, the Scottish physician who attended George III during his many years of illness. Cotswold Farm was the home of the 19th-century Methodist, Elizabeth Cross, who set up a mission in Tonga and converted the Tonga royal family. Duntisbourne Leer is prettily forded by the Dunt, as is Middle Duntisbourne, barely more than a farm at the bottom of a steep valley. The church at Duntisbourne Rouse has a particularly dramatic situation at the top of a slope leading down to the Dunt and an atmospheric interior with box pews and medieval wall paintings.

DURSLEY

Although this busy market town just beneath the Cotswold edge has been modernised in places, its old centre remains intact and boasts some interesting items. Nestling just beneath wooded slopes, it was once an important cloth manufacturing town and the delightfully arcaded market hall, built in 1729, and the Georgian Market House (town hall) sits bang in the centre, complete with statue of Queen Anne.

The church is not blessed with a very harmonious interior but does have a fine vaulted porch in the Perpendicular style. The tower in Gothic style was only rebuilt at the beginning of the 18th century with a grant from Queen Anne after the spire collapsed in 1698. The north door of the church was blocked to prevent its use as a right of way

for the collection of water from the Broad Well. Although in the immediate area Woodmancote offers a better selection of 18th-century houses, Dursley is a pleasant, old-fashioned sort of place and exploration of its centre is rewarding.

The village of Cam, just to the north of Dursley, still has a single factory producing high quality cloth, mostly for dress uniforms and for snooker table coverings. Cam church, apparently built by Lord Berkeley to save his soul after the murder of Edward II at Berkeley Castle, contains a Jacobean pulpit. The nearby Cam Peak and Cam Long Down are Cotswold outliers, which clearly show their geological formation, the softer rock having eroded around them.

Just to the northwest of Dursley is Stinchcombe Hill, the most westerly point of the Cotswolds. From its summit, Drakestone Point, there are far-reaching views along the escarpment to the Forest of Dean and the River Severn.

DYRHAM

A short distance to the north of Bath is Dyrham, a pretty village bearing a name associated with a battle of great consequence for Britain. In AD 577, on nearby Hinton Hill, the invading Anglo-Saxons defeated the Britons, forcing them into the mountains of Wales and permitting the capture of the Romano-British cities of Bath, Cirencester and Gloucester. Hinton Hill is covered in medieval plough furrows but there's no trace of the battle.

Dyrham Park was a Tudor house substantially rebuilt at the end of the 17th century for William Blathwayt. Now a National Trust property, it contains magnificent collections of china and Dutch paintings of the period, a reflection of the regular journeys that Blathwayt made to Holland in the company of William III. In the garden is one of the earliest-known greenhouses, while all that remains of the once elaborate water garden in the formal Dutch style is a statue of Neptune.

Insight

MINCHINHAMPTON COMMON

After the common was granted to the people of Minchinhampton in the 16th century, any weaver was permitted to enclose land here and build a home. The bulwarks are the remains of an Iron Age fort, and the possible base for the resistance to the Romans led by Caratacus; while Whitefield's Tump is a barrow from where George Whitefield, the Gloucester-born Methodist preacher addressed a 20,000-strong congregation in 1743. During World War I the common was used as an airfield by Australian airmen.

A herd of fallow deer now grazes in the parkland, as they have done since Saxon times, though now the park rejoices in the more naturalistic English style, designed by the great landscape architect Humphry Repton. In 1993 the house was a location in *Remains of the Day* which starred Sir Anthony Hopkins. The parkland is open all year.

MINCHINHAMPTON

Overlooking the Stroud Valley on the fringe of the eponymous common, Minchinhampton, one of the most important cloth towns of south Gloucestershire by the 18th century, easily goes unheeded. It was a town of small traders unable to withstand the various crashes that periodically afflicted the industry, and so finally relapsing to a rural calm. Indeed, the church's truncated tower may be explained by the absence of wealthy patrons to replace the decayed spire.

It deserves a look, however, for it is an attractive wool town built around the old Market Square. Here you'll find a 17th-century Market House balanced on stone pillars and, unusually, the post office residing in a Queen Anne building.

The church, just apart from the square, dates back to the 12th century. It contains a particularly fine set of brasses, while the 14th-century south transept contains a stately array of tombs and effigies.

The common is 600 acres (243ha) of National Trust owned turf. A wide, windswept expanse of grassland, fringed with the villages of the Frome and Nailsworth valleys, a circumnavigation of the common is rewarding for the views it reveals.

Amberley on the west side of the common, is featured in the Victorian novel, *John Halifax, Gentleman* by Mrs Craik. She lived at Rose Cottage.

NORTHLEACH

One of the most important of the wool towns in the Middle Ages, Northleach retains something of the flavour of that period, with its market square overlooked by one of the finest wool churches in the Cotswolds. It is all now bypassed by the A40 road, replacing the old coaching route which, in the past, ran through the town. The High Street is an interesting mixture of houses of all periods, some of which, are half-timbered and most of which reflect the burgage plots that belonged to the merchants of yore.

One of these buildings, just east of the market place, is now Keith Harding's World of Mechanical Music, in what was the old school. This is a fascinating place, a shop as you go in, but beyond it a collection of clocks and mechanical instruments from all over Europe, ranging from barrel organs to pianolas. Entertainingly, many of these are demonstrated, while some of the restored items are for sale.

Behind the square, among a little network of lanes about the old mill, is the most striking building in the town, its wool church which, as it stands, dates from the 15th century. A fine example of the English Perpendicular style, it is particularly noted for its south porch, one of the finest in the country. The interior is stark but beautifully proportioned and contains the grandest collection of monumental brasses in the Cotswolds, commemorating the medieval wool merchants who brought prosperity to Northleach and whose money was given to

PAINSWICK BEACON

Insight

BURGAGE PLOTS

Burgage plots were created to enable the maximum number of shops to line the main street. Northleach Borough was established by the Abbey of St Peter, in Gloucester, in 1226. The annual rents were one shilling (5p) for a burgage plot, 6d (2.5p) for a market stall and 1d for a cottage. These medieval property boundaries can still be traced.

build the church. There are two sets of almshouses, one at Mill End, another at East End. At the western end of town the High Street meets Roman Fosse Way. On the other side of the road is an 18th-century building that was originally a prison. The prison was built by Sir William Blackburn according to the ideas of the philanthropist Sir George Onesiphorus Paul, a member of an eminent family of Woodchester clothiers. The courthouse was in use until 1974. Just a short drive (or walk) to the northwest is the hamlet of Hampnett, which has an interesting Norman church with fine carved birds on the chancel arch and Victorian stencilling.

PAINSWICK

'The Queen of the Cotswolds' sits more or less at the point of transition from the northern to the southern Cotswolds. Perched regally at the edge of the steep slopes of the Painswick Valley, the town is a hive of activity about the little network of lanes around the church. It is the most Dickensian in character of the Cotswold villages. Like other important towns in the area, Painswick's prosperity reached its peak in the 17th and 18th centuries when the stream below was harnessed to work the mills producing wool cloth. The pure water also meant that cloth dyeing became important. The character of the village depends considerably on the fine houses built by the wealthy wool merchants of the era.

PAINSWICK

But the most striking feature is the graceful 17th-century spire of the church. The church itself is mainly 15th century and contains some interesting monuments, although it is the churchyard for which Painswick is especially noted. There are two reasons for this. The most striking features are the clipped colonnades of yew, which have graced the churchyard since 1792. There are said to be only 99, since the Devil always kills off the hundredth, and indeed, it is now impossible to count them with ease since some have become intertwined with each other.

The other distinction are table tombs from the 17th and 18th centuries, many of which were carved by a local mason, Joseph Bryan, and his two sons.

Stroll around the heart of the town and along Bisley Street, the original main street and the oldest part of the town. Here you will find the Little Fleece, now a National Trust bookshop in a largely 17th-century house that was built onto the 14th-century Fleece Inn.

Just outside the town, on the Gloucester road, is Painswick Rococo Garden, the landscaped 18th-century garden around Painswick House. It is utterly

Insight

THE CLYPPING CEREMONY

The Clypping Ceremony at Painswick church has nothing to do with pruning the famous yew trees in the churchyard but derives from the Old English word 'clyppan', meaning to embrace. It takes place every 19 September, or the nearest Sunday, in association with the Feast of the Nativity of St Mary. In the afternoon the children involved in the ceremony join hands to form a circle around the church, approach the church and retreat three times as they sing a traditional hymn. A special cake is also baked – known as 'puppy dog pie', it contains a small china dog, a reminder, perhaps, of the pagan origins of the festivity.

Visit

THE ORPHEUS PAVEMENT

The Visitor Centre at Prinknash Abbey houses a beautiful reconstruction of a superb Roman mosaic that was found in a churchyard in North Woodchester, near Stroud. This original was badly damaged, and not easy for visitors to see, so the decision was made never to unearth it again, but rather to build a reconstruction. It was originally made by mosaicists from Cirencester in around AD 325 and tells the story of Orpheus, who charmed the natural world with the music of his lyre.

charming, particularly in early spring when snowdrops flower in abundance. Nearby is Painswick Beacon, site of an Iron Age fort known as Kimsbury Camp and a golf course, from where there are views across the plain to Gloucester.

The neighbouring villages of Sheepscombe and Slad are noted for their associations with the *Cider With Rosie* author Laurie Lee.

PRINKNASH

Close to Painswick on the sheltered slopes beneath Cranham Woods is a building which, despite looking like a huge cinema, just about succeeds in blending in with its surroundings, a testament to the use of good building materials, in this case stone from the quarries around Guiting. Prinknash (pronounced 'Prinash'), a Benedictine house, is one of Britain's few abbeys. The 16th-century foundation, a hunting lodge for the abbots of Gloucester, became a manor house and chapel. It was used as his headquarters by Prince Rupert during the Siege of Gloucester and is still visible across the valley. Its location was celebrated by Horace Walpole who, in 1714, described it as 'commanding Elysium'. The last private owner was a Catholic who invited the monks to move here from Caldey Island, off the Welsh coast. The current building was begun in 1939. The abbey is worth visiting for its magnificent views, the tea room, the Orpheus Pavement, the abbey church and the gardens. The nearby Bird and Deer Park is well stocked with birds, goats and deer.

THE SODBURYS

There are in fact three Sodburys – Little, Old and Chipping – scattered around narrow lanes down the Cotswold escarpment, with a remote character that hardly seems part of the Cotswolds, and in fact has more in common with the vale. Chipping Sodbury (Chipping, as elsewhere, here means 'market') is the newest of the villages, deliberately established to become a market town in 1227. More recently, J K Rowling, author of the Harry Potter books, was born here. Old Sodbury, the original, has an ancient church and a Bronze to Iron Age encampment above the town from where there are magnificent views. Little Sodbury is the most interesting of the three. Small as it is, this village has a rich history. Gloucestershire-born scholar

William Tyndale (c1494–1536), the translator of the Bible into English, came to the manor house in 1521 as tutor and chaplain. A few years later, Henry VIII and Anne Boleyn stayed in the house, which has a wonderful 15th-century Great Hall.

The church, dedicated to St Adeline, originally stood next to the manor house but was moved to its present site when urgent repairs had to be carried out. Near the Sodburys is the Somerset, or Hawkesbury, Monument, erected in 1846. This commemorates Lord Edward Somerset, one of the Badminton Beauforts. He served at the Battle of Waterloo with exceptional gallantry for which he received thanks from the government of the day.

SOUTH CERNEY & THE COTSWOLD WATER PARK

South Cerney, 3 miles (4.8km) southeast of Cirencester, sits on the banks of the Churn, where you will find rows of very attractive cottages along Silver Street and Church Lane. The church has a Norman south doorway with sculptures above, reflecting Heaven and Hell, while within are the remains of a 12th-century crucifix, one of the earliest wood carvings in the country.

The old Thames and Severn Canal passes just to the north of the village and walks along the tow-path are possible; but the village is best known for the series of flooded gravel pits that make up the Cotswold Water Park. Broadly speaking there are two sections,

one between Cricklade and Kemble (where South Cerney is situated), the other between Fairford and Lechlade, which provide facilities for nature lovers, bird watchers and sports-lovers alike. There are seven nature reserves and the wetlands attract millions of wildfowl, particularly in the winter. Miraculously, the various activities coexist happily on 140 lakes.

THE STROUD VALLEY

For a small area, the Cotswolds reveal remarkable natural diversity, but the Stroud Valley possesses a singular character, much dependent on its depth, narrow base and serpentine course. Stroud itself is at the head of the valley, which runs east close to Cirencester, a number of other valleys feeding it from north and south.

Its character is also dependent upon its history as the manufacturing centre of the Cotswolds, with its fast-flowing streams and the mills that straddled

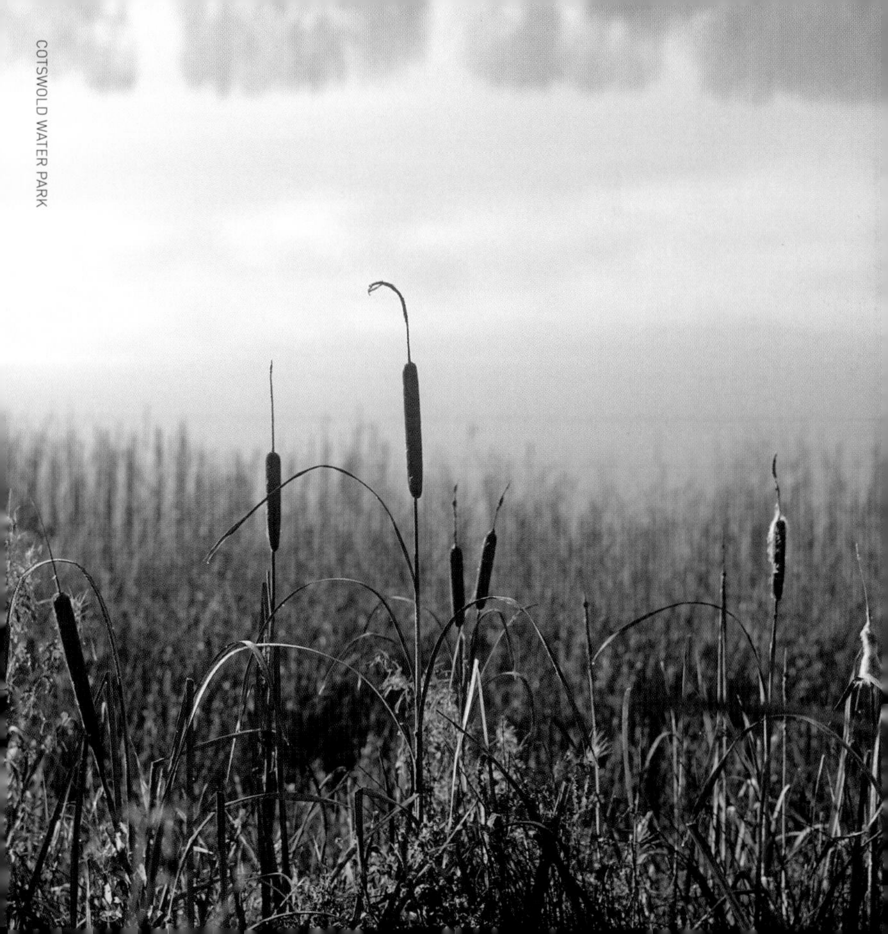

COTSWOLD WATER PARK

Insight

ARTS AND CRAFTS MOVEMENT

The Arts and Crafts Movement, a London and Cotswold phenomenon, was a 19th-century aesthetic and social movement instigated by the art critic John Ruskin and the artist and poet William Morris as a constructive protest against the mass-produced excesses of the Industrial Revolution. A company, Morris & Co., was established to produce hand-made furniture, glass, wallpapers and textiles. It looked to the Middle Ages for its ideal and liked to concentrate on fine materials, solid craftsmanship and expertise and a certain simplicity of style that was both rustic and courtly, of universal appeal. Later, in 1888, Morris helped the artist and designer C R Ashbee to found the Guild and School of Arts and Crafts, but production costs led to its early demise. However, some of the designs, particularly for textiles and wallpaper, remain popular and the tradition of quality workmanship continues to inspire craftsmen in the area.

them. Stroud became the centre of the wool industry from the 15th century as cloth supplanted fleece in importance. With industrialisation during the 18th and 19th centuries the valley bristled with mills. There were 150 of them at one time, before decline set in as the industry moved away to Yorkshire, leaving only two companies producing high-quality cloth for dress uniforms.

Stroud itself is spread a little like a cloth over the Cotswold slopes. Of no great beauty, it is nonetheless a bustling town of considerable interest, centred in the area around the High Street, close to which you will find the Shambles, the former meat market, and the Tudor Town Hall. Close by, on George Street, are the handsome 19th-century Subscription Rooms, home to the Tourist Information Centre. The Museum in the Park, which is situated next to the Stratford Park Leisure Centre, offers an excellent insight into the history of the area and interesting displays, among other items, a collection of early lawnmowers (the inventor of the lawnmower, Mr Budding, was from the Stroud Valley).

There are some good walks to be enjoyed along the Stroudwater Canal, once the more successful part of the Thames and Severn Canal system, functioning until 1954, and now being restored.

Southwest of Stroud lies Selsley Common and Selsley, with its church of particular interest for its stained glass by William Morris, Philip Webb, Dante Gabriel Rossetti, Edward Burne-Jones and Ford Madox Brown. Just farther west, near Stonehouse, is one of the area's pre-industrial legacies, Frocester Tithe Barn, one of the finest in England.

To the east of Stroud is Chalford, its houses on steep lanes and along terraces and shelves of the north slope of the valley. A legacy of the Industrial Revolution, its houses were built by the clothiers and merchants making their fortune during the 18th and 19th centuries

and by weavers working first from home and later at the mills that still line the Thames and Severn Canal. The 18th-century church contains several items produced by members of the Arts and Crafts Movement.

The Thames and Severn Canal, today the subject of a restoration project, was one of those great Victorian enterprises that was magnificent in conception but almost redundant by the time of its realisation. Completed in 1789, to facilitate trade between the two rivers that were also important commercial waterways, the number of locks, problems with the size of the 2.25-mile (3.6km) Sapperton Tunnel and a shortage of water engendered constant problems. Other, better, canals and the arrival of the railways put paid to it and the last recorded journey was made in 1911. The two temple-like tunnel portals are visible at Coates and Daneway where the pubs, built for the boatmen, still function. A stroll along the old canal is recommended,

as indeed is a visit to the village of Sapperton, the home of Ernest Gimson and the Barnsley brothers, of the Arts and Crafts Movement.

Just to the north of Chalford is Bisley village, with pubs and a church that has a dramatic spire and, in the churchyard, a unique 'Poor Soul's Light', a 13th-century structure that contained candles lit during masses for the poor.

South of Stroud at Woodchester, is the site of a Roman villa with a magnificent mosaic. This fine Orpheus mosaic is the largest in Britain. Woodchester Mansion lies south of Woodchester on the road to Dursley. It is a fascinating place to visit as the house was abandoned by its builders in the mid 1870s before it could be completed. It is preserved in the state it was left.

To the south, just outside Nailsworth, is the fascinating Dunkirk Mill, where a massive overshot waterwheel can be seen, together with a well-presented history of the local textile industry.

Activity

RODBOROUGH COMMON

Rodborough Common is just to the south-west of Stroud. A good place for walking, the common is also the site of Rodborough Fort, built in 1761 as a pleasure-house by George Hawker, a local dyer. It was rebuilt in Victorian style in 1870.

TETBURY

This is a small, quiet market town of some charm, set among the broader slopes of the southern Cotswolds, on a promontory overlooking a tributary of the River Avon.

By the 18th century Tetbury was one of the most important cloth market towns of south Gloucestershire. Its main streets radiate from the impressive market square, dominated by the 17th-century Town Hall or Market House, resting on three rows of tubby Etruscan pillars, but reduced by one storey in 1817. The square is also noted for the Snooty Fox Hotel.

The road next to the Snooty Fox leads to Chipping Steps and the site of the old livestock market, surrounded by some handsome 18th- and 19th-century houses and the Old Priory. The road continues down to the foot of Gumstool Hill, the scene for the annual Woolsack Races on Millennium Green on Spring Bank Holiday Monday.

South from the square, along Church Street, is the magnificent St Mary's Church, rebuilt in Gothic style in the late 18th century. The spire is 186 feet (57m) tall. The interior, lit by Perpendicular-style windows, is coolly elegant. Rows of box pews, with their own entries from the ambulatories, are presided over by panelled galleries and two splendid chandeliers. The church is the home of the Tetbury Heritage Centre.

Tetbury has an unusual museum, at the western end of Long Street, which runs west out of Market Square. The Police Museum is housed in the cells of the Old Court House and displays police memorabilia such as uniforms on loan from Gloucestershire Constabulary.

Just over a mile (1.6km) to the northwest of Tetbury is Chavenage, a delightful manor where Cromwell stayed during his attempt to persuade the owner to accede to the execution of Charles I. There is an collection of 17th-century tapestries. The chapel, with a Saxon font found in an estate barn, is close by. Four miles (6.4km) to the northeast, stands Rodborough Manor, a fine example of a house built in the traditional Arts and Crafts style.

Three miles (4.8km) southwest of Tetbury is Westonbirt Arboretum, where more than 18,000 trees thrive in 600 acres (243ha) of glade and 17 miles (27.2km) of footpaths. The Arboretum was started in 1829 by Sir Robert Holford of Westonbirt House. This is a 19th-century neo-Elizabethan building designed by Lewis Vulliamy, who also designed the Snooty Fox in Tetbury and London's Dorchester Hotel.

ULEY & OWLPEN

Uley, a large and pretty village of 18th-century houses that scuttle down the hillside into a deep valley, became prosperous through the wool dyeing industry, famous for its 'Uley Blue'. There is still a functioning brewery, while the Crown is a fine pub. Uley Bury overlooks the town – it is a classic hill-fort site, a flat 32-acre (13ha) plateau surrounded by steep slopes. It was occupied by the Dobunni, the native tribe overrun by the Romans, but there are indications of occupation during Neolithic times. A short walk is recommended for its fine views.

North of Uley, towards Frocester Hill, is Hetty Pegler's Tump – the unusual name comes from the 17th-century landowner's wife. This 180-foot (55m) Neolithic barrow, surrounded by a stone wall, has a long central chamber that can be entered, with some discomfort, by obtaining the key from a nearby cottage. It may be wise to take a torch. East of Uley, within striking distance by foot, is Owlpen Manor, a very picturesque 15th-century manor house restored in the 1920s, displaying a good collection of Arts and Crafts furniture. Close by is the 19th-century church and 18th-century mill.

One mile (1.6km) east of Owlpen is a tranquil garden at Kingscote called Matara. Eastern and Western ideas of garden design are blended to produce a very restful place.

Activity

WESTONBIRT ARBORETUM

Managed by the Forestry Commission, Westonbirt Arboretum contains one of the most important collections of trees and shrubs in the world and is beautiful at any time of year – marvellous displays of flowers in spring, shady glades in summer, the mellow russets and yellows of autumn and the Siberian grandeur of winter. The arboretum has excellent facilities including a visitor centre, café, restaurant, picnic area, plant centre and shop.

OWLPEN

WOTTON-UNDER-EDGE

Wotton-under-Edge is perhaps one of the most interesting small towns in the Cotswolds. In the Middle Ages Wotton was an important wool town entitled to hold markets and fairs and the Chipping, part of which is now a car park, was the site for them. The old fire station in the Chipping is now an interesting heritage centre, showing the history of the town and the surrounding area. From the Chipping, Market Street leads past the Star Inn and the Town Hall, to a junction with High Street and Long Street.

On the corner of Market Street and High Street there is the smart red brick Tolsey, granted to the town in 1595 by the Countess of Warwick to serve as a market court. Overlooking the High Street from the other side of Haw Street is the old police station.

Long Street, the main shopping thoroughfare, which is lined with an array of architectural styles, has a lot of character. A stroll along Orchard Street on the right will bring you to the home of Isaac Pitman, inventor of shorthand. At the end of Long Street turn left into Church Street, opposite the 17th-century Falcon Hotel. On the right is a row of delightful almshouses, built in 1638. If you choose, go into the courtyard and visit the little chapel, lit by a pair of depictive stained-glass windows.

Church Street then crosses over Old Town to Culverhay, bringing you to the 18th-century Church Hall, former home to the Blue Coat Church of England School, and the entrance to the parish church, consecrated in 1283, though most of the building is 15th-century. Beyond the churchyard is Potters Pond where the Ram Inn, dating from 1350, is thought to be the oldest building here.

Just over a mile (1.6km) to the east at Ozleworth stands Newark Park, owned by the National Trust, an unusual 16th-century house built as a hunting lodge, with magnificent views across the countryside.

TOURIST INFORMATION OFFICES

Bath
Abbey Chambers, Abbey Churchyard.
Tel: 01225 477101;
www.visitbath.co.uk

Cirencester
Corn Hall, Market Place.
Tel: 01285 654180

Northleach
Cotswold Heritage Centre.
Tel: 01451 860715

Painswick
The Library, Stroud Road.
Tel: 01452 813552

Stroud
Subscription Rooms, George Street.
Tel: 01453 760960

Tetbury
33 Church Street.
Tel: 01666 503552

PLACES OF INTEREST

Arlington Mill Museum
Bibury. Tel: 01285 740199

Barnsley House Garden
Barnsley. Tel: 01285 740000

Bath Abbey Heritage Vaults
Tel: 01225 422462

Bath Postal Museum
27 Northgate Street. Tel: 01225 460333;
www.bathpostalmuseum.org

Beckford's Tower and Museum
Lansdown Road, Bath.
Tel: 01225 460705;
www.bath-preservation-trust.org.uk

Building of Bath Museum
The Vineyards, The Paragon, Bath.
Tel: 01225 333895;
www.bath-preservation-trust.org.uk

Buscot Park
Buscot. Tel: 01367 240786;
www.buscot-park.com

Cerney House Gardens
North Cerney. Tel: 01285 831205;
www.cerneygardens.com

Chedworth Roman Villa
Chedworth. Tel: 01242 890256;
www.nationaltrust.org.uk

Compton Cassey Gallery
Compton Cassey House, nr Withington.
Tel: 01242 890224;
www.jonathanpoole.co.uk

Corinium Museum
Park Street, Cirencester.
Tel: 01285 655611;
 www.cotswold.gov.uk/go/museum

Dunkirk Mill Centre
Stroud. Tel: 01453 766273;
www.stroud-textile.org.uk

Dyrham Park
Dyrham. Tel: 0117 9372501;
www.nationaltrust.org.uk

Heritage Centre
The Chipping, Wotton-under-Edge.
Tel: 01453 521541;
www.wottonheritage.com

Holburne Museum of Art
Great Pulteney Street, Bath.
Tel: 01225 466669;
www.bath.ac.uk/holburne

Jane Austen Centre
Gay Street, Bath.
Tel: 01225 443000;
www.janeausten.co.uk

Matara Gardens
Kingscote Park, Kingscote.
Tel: 01453 861050;
www.matara.co.uk

Medieval Hall
High Street, Stroud.

Museum in the Park
Stratford Park, Stroud.
Tel: 01453 763394;
www.stroud.gov.uk/museum

Number 1, Royal Crescent
Bath. Tel: 01225 428126;
www.bath-preservation-trust.org.uk

Newark Park
Ozleworth, Wotton-under-Edge.
Tel: 01453 842644;
www.nationaltrust.org.uk

Owlpen Manor
Uley. Tel: 01453 860261;
www.owlpen.com

Painswick Rococo Garden
Gloucester Road, Painswick.
Tel: 01452 813204;
www.rococogarden.co.uk

**Prinknash Abbey, The Orpheus
Roman Pavement**
Nr Cranham.Tel: 01452 812066;
www.prinknashabbey.org.uk

Prinknash Bird and Deer Park
Tel: 01452 812727; www.prinknash-
bird-and-deerpark.com

Roman Baths Museum
Stall Street, Bath. Tel: 01225 477785;
www.romanbaths.co.uk

Ruskin Mill College
Mill Bottom, Nailsworth.
Tel: 01453 832571;
www.ruskin-mill.org.uk

Tetbury Police Museum
The Old Courthouse, 63 Long Street.
Tel: 01666 504670; www.tetbury.org

Thermae Bath Spa
Hot Bath Street, Bath.
Tel: 01225 331234;
www.thermaebathspa.com

Victoria Art Gallery
Bridge Street, Bath.
Tel: 01225 477233; www.victoriagal.org.

Westonbirt Arboretum
Tel: 01666 880220. Open all year, daily.

William Herschel Museum
19 New King Street, Bath.
Tel: 01225 446865;
www.bath-preservation-trust.org.uk

Woodchester Mansion
Nympsfield. Tel: 01453 861541;
www.woodchestermansion.org.uk

Wotton-under-Edge Heritage Centre
The Chipping, Wotton-under-Edge.
Tel: 01453 521541;
www.wottonheritage.com

FOR CHILDREN
Butts Farm Visitor Centre
Nr South Cerney. Tel: 01285 869414;
www.buttsfarmshop.com

Countryside Centre
Bath Road, Haresfield.
Tel: 01452 728338

Norwood Farm
Bath Road, Norton St Philip.
Tel: 01373 834356;
www.norwoodfarm.co.uk

Prinknash Bird and Deer Park
Tel: 01452 812727; www.prinknash-bird-and-deerpark.com

SHOPPING
Bath
Farmers' Market, first and second Sats,
Green Park Station; market at Twerton,
Thu, and Old Down, Sat.

Cirencester
Farmers' Market, second and fourth
Sat; street market, Mon and Fri, both
held in the Market Place.

Dursley
Market, Fri.

Fairford
Market, Wed.

Stroud
Farmers' Market, first and third Sat,
Corn Hill Market.
Market, Wed, Fri and Sat.

Tetbury
Market, Wed.

LOCAL SPECIALITIES
Crafts
Brewery Arts Centre, Cirencester.
Tel: 01285 657181;
www.breweryarts.org.uk
Pottery
Lansdown Pottery, Stroud.
Tel: 01453 753051;
www.lansdownpottery.org

PERFORMING ARTS
Cotswold Playhouse
Parliament Street, Stroud.
Tel: 0870 432 5405
Theatre Royal
Sawclose, Bath.
Tel: 01225 448844;
www.theatreroyal.org.uk

OUTDOOR ACTIVITIES
BOAT TRIPS
Bath
Pride of Bath, North Parade Bridge.
Tel: 01225 331647;
www.prideofbath.com

COUNTRY PARKS
Avon Valley Country Park, Keynsham.
Tel: 0117 9864929;
www.avonvalleycountrypark.co.uk
CYCLE HIRE
Bath
Bath and Dundas Canal Co, Monkton Combe.
Tel: 01225 722292;
www.bathcanal.com

ANNUAL EVENTS & CUSTOMS
Badminton
Badminton Horse Trials, May.
Bath
Literature Festival, Feb or Mar; Music Festival, May/Jun.
Mozartfest, Nov.
Cirencester
Cotswold Country Fair, Jul.
Fairford
Royal International Air Tattoo, Jul.
Gatcombe
Horse Trials, Jul or Aug.
Painswick
Church Clypping Ceremony, late Sep.

TEA ROOMS

Sally Lunn's
4 North Parade Passage,
Bath, BA1 1NX
Tel: 01225 461634
www.sallylunns.co.uk
The famous Sally Lunn Bun was
originally baked in Georgian times and
is still on offer in this historic tea shop
in the oldest house in Bath.

Arlington Mill Tea Shop
Arlington Mill, Bibury, GL7 5NL
Tel: 01285 740199
An old mill now houses an idiosyncratic
shop, museum and a good tea shop.
Choose from all-day breakfasts, light
lunches (with trout from the Bibury
Trout Farm next door) and cream teas.

Tollgate Tea Shop
Oldfield Gatehouse,
Dyrham Park, SN14 8ER
Tel: 01225 891585
Visit this stone building with arched
windows for teas served in a very
welcoming atmosphere. No artificial
ingredients are used in their excellent
cakes and scones.

Ruskin Mill
Old Bristol Road, Nailsworth, GL6 0LA
Tel: 01453 837537
www.ruskin-mill.org.uk
Make time, when visiting this vibrant
art and craft centre, to enjoy tea with
a piece of organic cake before a stroll
round the gardens and the ponds.

Hobbs House
4 George Street, Nailsworth, GL6 0AG
Tel: 01453 839396
www.hobbshousebakery.co.uk
This innovative café, which
is one of Rick Stein's Food Heroes,
sells an amazing range of breads and
patisserie using excellent and locally
sourced ingredients.

BIBURY

The New Inn at Coln
Coln St Aldwyns, GL7 5AN
Tel: 01285 750651
www.new-inn.co.uk
One of the prettiest villages in the Cotswolds is home to this attractive inn. Eat in the bar, or in the flower-filled courtyard, or, for a superb meal, try the restaurant.

The Green Dragon Inn
Cockleford, Cowley, GL53 9NW
Tel: 01242 870271
www.green-dragon-inn.co.uk
Tucked away in a small hamlet, this charming 17th-century stone inn offers peace and relaxation. One of the bars has work by Robert Thompson, with his famous trademark mice carved into the furniture and fittings. The menu here is extensive, and there are good wines.

The Crown Inn
Frampton Mansell, GL6 8GJ
Tel: 01285 760681
Surrounded by the beauty of the Golden Valley, this old inn is full of low beams and has cosy open fireplaces. In warm weather, there is plenty of seating in the garden. Fresh, local food is served in the restaurant and in the three inviting bars.

The Weighbridge Inn
Minchinhampton, GL6 9AL
Tel: 01453 835903
www.2in1pub.co.uk
This former weighbridge is full of interesting local memorabilia. It is most famous, however, for its 2-in-1 pies, with home-made cauliflower cheese as one part and the meat or fish filling of your choice.

Eastern Cotswolds

INTRODUCTION

The distinctive character of the Cotswolds spills over into the surrounding counties of Gloucestershire, Oxfordshire and Warwickshire, where charming villages of honeyed limestone (with equally charming names), such as Minster Lovell and Chipping Norton can be found amid rolling pastures. Also in this area is Blenheim Palace, a World Heritage Site, which has vast gardens and is famous as the birthplace of Winston Churchill. Kelmscott Manor, on the edge of Kelmscot village, is a 16th-century, limestone farmhouse set in lovely gardens.

Unmissable attractions

Explore magnificent Blenheim Palace, a World Heritage Site, which has vast gardens and is famous as the birthplace of Winston Churchill…enjoy Kelmscott Manor on the edge of Kelmscot, a 16th-century limestone farmhouse set in idyllic gardens and the home of William Morris…admire the dovecote at the charming village of Minster Lovell…explore Chipping Norton, a busy market town with a rich history…hire a boat and float down the river at Lechlade…visit the ancient Rollright Stones…discover fascinating villages set long the Windrush Valley – Witney, Sherborne and Swinbrook.

1 Blenheim Palace
The grounds of Blenheim Palace are a perfect setting for the superb building, designed by the genius Sir John Vanburgh.

2 Kelmscott Manor
William Morris, founder of the Arts and Crafts movement, lived at the manor for 25 years. The property is a showcase for the ideals and work of the movement.

3 Dovecote, Minster Lovell
The circular medieval dovecote has been well maintained, revealing its intricate construction.

COTSWOLDS

Area of Outstanding
Natural Beauty

BURFORD

BURFORD

Just off the main Oxford road, Burford is all but invisible to passing motorists. Drive north from the roundabout, however, and almost immediately, from the brow of the ridge, Burford slips away before you in a sedate cascade of handsome inns and charming cottages. The wide main street, lined with good shops and pubs, passes the church to the right before crossing the Windrush on a medieval bridge of 1322, by the old mill.

Burford's prosperity over the centuries has depended on three factors – wool, quarrying and coaching. There were burgesses here in the 13th century and the town grew rapidly to become an important wool centre.

The nearby quarries at the Barringtons, Upton and especially Taynton produced some of the most notable stone in the Cotswolds. Much of that stone was used in the construction of some of England's finest buildings – Blenheim Palace,

Visit

ROYAL APPOINTMENT

Burford was also famous for its saddlery business. This was in part, at least, a result of the proximity of the Bibury races, which used to take place on the course near Aldsworth. Burford saddles received an unspoken royal appointment as a result of the visits of Charles II and his mistress Nell Gwynn who used to stay here when the races were on.

St Paul's Cathedral and various Oxford colleges. The Barringtons also produced the Strongs, a family of masons – Sir Thomas Strong was Christopher Wren's master mason in the construction of St Paul's Cathedral. Another eminent family of masons, the Kempsters, came from Upton and Burford.

A fillip for Burford came with the dawn of the coaching era from the 18th century, when the town was an important stop on the route to Oxford and London. This, however, came

Insight

SIMON WYSDOM

Opposite the almshouses are the old buildings of Burford Grammar School, founded in 1577 by a wealthy cloth merchant, Simon Wysdom. He was also responsible for the construction of the Weavers' Cottages, which are grouped near the medieval bridge.

to an end with the railway, which happened to bypass Burford.

Burford is a delight to stroll about. While the High Street is the main thoroughfare, Sheep Street to the west, and Witney Street and Church Lane to the east, have much to offer. Along Sheep Street there are some very fine inns – the Bay Tree Hotel and the Lamb Inn (the old brewery next door houses the Tourist Information Centre) – while Witney Street boasts perhaps the finest building in the town, the 17th-century Great House, possibly built by the local mason Christopher Kempster. From Witney Street, Guildenford leads to Church Lane where there is a row of lovely almshouses, founded in 1457, are close to St John the Baptist church.

The 15th-century parish church is impressive. Among the chapels and monuments, perhaps the finest is the one erected in 1628 to Sir Lawrence Tanfield, Lord Chief Baron of the Exchequer to James I. Another fine memorial, to Edmund Harman, barber-surgeon to Henry VIII, includes the first representation in Britain of Amazonian Indians from the New World. On the rim of the font the autograph of a Leveller, one of 340 Roundhead mutineers kept here for three days during the Civil War, is inscribed: 'Anthony Sedley prisner 1649' (sic). From the High Street, near the bridge, Priory Lane takes you past Elizabethan Priory, which now houses a Benedictine Anglican community.

Back on the High Street, on the corner of Sheep Street, is the pillared Tolsey, a Tudor house where

wool merchants used to meet and which now houses a museum of great interest. Further down is the wide arch of the old George Hotel where Charles I used to stay with Nell Gwynn and which later became an important coaching inn. Their son was created Earl of Burford.

Three miles (4.8km) south of Burford are the Cotswold Wildlife Park and Gardens, which are set in the grounds of a 19th-century mansion. The varied collection consists of animals from all over the world, with tropical birds, reptiles, an aquarium, insect house and children's farmyard. The gardens, including tropical plants, are continually improving.

CHARLBURY

Here is a town that is unexpected in a number of ways. This area of the Cotswolds hides its villages well in its folds and Charlbury is a small, busy town that looks across the Evenlode valley in happy isolation towards Wychwood Forest.

It seems to be self-sufficient, more or less, with a large number of shops, inns and a railway station (designed by Isambard Kingdom Brunel). Although Charlbury was a sheep town in the past, it was also renowned as a centre of glove manufacture. At the height of its prosperity, in the mid-19th century, more than 1,000 people were employed in the industry.

Behind the main street is a delightful small green called the Playing Close, which is surrounded by handsome villas and cottages,

Insight

LITERARY ASSOCIATIONS

Finstock, a couple of miles (3.2km) south of Charlbury, has several literary associations. The great poet T S Eliot was baptised into the church here in 1927, while the novelist Barbara Pym, who died in 1980, lived here for the last eight years of her life.

and solid iron railings looking across to a handsome Jacobean-style drinking fountain at one end.

Charlbury's church, on the other side of the main street, is largely Perpendicular in style, with Norman pillars and arches on the north side, but otherwise with a rather Victorian interior. The town museum in Market Street is dedicated to the traditional crafts and industries of the area

Beyond the River Evenlode is Cornbury Park, an extravagant gift from Elizabeth I to her favourite, for a time, Robert Dudley. A pleasant walk can be had through the

forested grounds of this largely 17th-century house, which will also take you across the approach bridge built in 1689. A National Nature Reserve forms part of the land and this, with the house, is not open to the public.

Ditchley Park, west of Charlbury, is only occasionally open to the public by appointment. The fine 18th-century mansion was built for the 2nd Earl of Lichfield by James Gibbs, while the landscaping is by 'Capability' Brown. The grounds consist of a 300-acre park, pleasant gardens, a lake, temples and woodland. The house was the historic meeting place of Winston Churchill and President Roosevelt during World War II.

CHIPPING NORTON

This busy market town, the highest in Oxfordshire at 646 feet (197m), is distinguished at its outskirts by the large Victorian tweed mill, now converted to flats, that sits in a fold to the west of the town. The Bliss Tweed Mill, built in 1872 by

CHARLBURY

Insight

CHURCHILL

Just 3 miles (4.8km) southwest of Chipping Norton, and close to Stow-on-the-Wold is the village of Churchill, the birthplace of Warren Hastings, the first Governor-General of India. It was also the birthplace of William Smith, 'the Father of English Geology', who produced the first geological map of England. Their stories are well told in the Churchill and Sarsden Heritage Centre in the Old Church, which also contains village records and maps dating back to the 17th century.

the Lancashire architect George Woodhouse, closed in 1980 and is an unusual reminder, in the Cotswolds, of the Industrial Revolution; and yet there is something disconcertingly memorable about this example of the Victorian age.

The heart of Chipping Norton is the fine Market Square which is dominated by the 19th-century Town Hall, with its Tuscan-style portico.

Opposite the Town Hall steps is the museum, which has displays on the town's history. Around the town you'll find a varied collection of shops, hotels and houses dating back to the 17th century, though most are 18th century – a testimony to former prosperity that the wool trade brought to Chipping Norton.

From the square, the town slopes down Church Street past a row of charming almshouses dating back to 1640 towards St Mary's, a Perpendicular church containing some fine brasses and impressive tombs. Its most unusual feature is the hexagonal porch with a vaulted ceiling. Behind the church are the motte-and-bailey earthworks that indicate that the town was already of some strategic or commercial importance in the Norman period.

In Middle Row look out for the 16th-century Guildhall. Chipping Norton is one of the few towns in the area blessed with a theatre, which is particularly well known for its well-acted pantomimes.

FAIRFORD

Fairford is most often thought of in connection with the supersonic airliner Concorde, which had its maiden flight at the military airfield here. Every year in July the Royal International Air Tattoo is held at RAF Fairford. But Fairford is more than an airfield. Located on the River Coln and the A417, Fairford is another of those towns that has a busy lowland feel, which does not seem to be entirely characteristic of the Cotswolds.

The focal point of the village, wherein lies its fame, is its magnificent late Perpendicular Church of St Mary, largely rebuilt from 1497 by John Tame and his son Edmund, the most influential of Fairford's medieval wool merchants. The parish church is dominated by a central tower supported by massive pillars within; but its greatest glory is the spectacular medieval stained-glass windows, the only complete set in the country, which narrate the highlights of the Biblical story.

Insight

QUARRY WORKERS

The last people to work some of the quarries in the Filkins' area, before they were reopened by George Swinford in 1929, were French prisoners of war from the Battle of Waterloo.

They are most likely the work of the Flanders craftsman, Barnard Flower, whom Henry VIII employed to glaze the windows of King's College Chapel, Cambridge and the Lady Chapel, Westminster Abbey, and who was almost certainly helped by English and French craftsmen. The great west window, in particular, which shows the Last Judgement, is of riveting, luminous beauty. Not to be missed either are the amusing carved misericords underneath the choir stalls. In the churchyard are buried two distinguished locals – Valentine Strong, of the eminent family of stone quarriers of Taynton; and Tiddles, the church cat.

The church overlooks the green water meadows and the old mill by a picturesque bridge. From the church a pleasant circuit is possible and will bring you back to the main street. Most of the houses that line the street are 17th or 18th century and, along with the many inns, are a reminder of Fairford's role as a coaching town. John Keble, the 19th-century church reformer, was born at Keble House, on the north side of the road at the east end of the town. To the north are the picturesque twin villages of Eastleach Turville and Eastleach Martin, which are separated by the River Leach.

Insight

LORD OF THE MANOR

The influence of the Tame family and the proximity of the river led Henry VIII's librarian, John Leland, to observe: 'Fairforde never flourished afore ye Tames came to it'. Wool merchant John Tame, who built Fairford's church, became Fairford's lord of the manor. His son, Sir Edmund Tame, is responsible for St Peter's at Rendcomb, 5 miles (8km) north of Cirencester, where his initials can be found on some of the corbels and on old glass in a nave window. It is thought that the church tower at Barnsley was largely the result of his patronage.

FILKINS

This is a quiet Cotswold village that has a distinctly bypassed feel. Its cottages are distinguished for their solid craftsmanship rather than their beauty, and their story can be read in an entertaining book, *Jubilee Boy*, (on sale at the woollen mill, among other places) by an ancient local resident, George Swinford. He worked as a foreman on the estate belonging to the British statesman, Sir Stafford Cripps, and has also given his name to Swinford Museum of Rural Life in the village.

Filkins village is best known, however, for its working woollen-weaving factory, one of the last, if not the last, in the Cotswolds, a rather

poignant fact when it is considered that the very landscape of the area owes its character to sheep. But Cotswold Woollen Weavers keeps the flag flying, producing quality clothes, on clattering old looms, to suit most tastes. The factory premises are an attractive old barn. All the processes of production can be watched and, while it is a serious business concern, the historical relevance of wool production is not overlooked, for there is a permanent exhibition devoted to sheep and wool. There is also a café, an art gallery and an excellent shop. Adjoining buildings contain more workshops devoted to other traditional crafts.

A short distance east of Filkins are some interesting little villages. The Norman south doorway of the church at Kencot dates back to the 12th century and is decorated with a carving of Sagittarius shooting an arrow into the mouth of a monster. The church at Alvescot set in a quiet location to the north of the village, has a fine 16th-century brass.

KELMSCOT

A small village, the fame of which is inseparable from the 19th-century poet and artist, William Morris. On the façade of a terrace of cottages on the main street, there he is in carved relief seated in the shade of a tree, knapsack and hat at his side. Kelmscott Manor, on the edge of the village, was his home from 1871 until his death in 1896. He is buried in the local churchyard in a grave, designed by Philip Webb and modelled on a Viking tomb.

Kelmscott Manor (limited public opening) was built in the late 16th century. Morris only rented it but it now contains a fine collection of items associated with the man and with his craft, most notably those comparatively simple, domestic artefacts that he strove to see reinvigorated through the Arts and Crafts Movement. It also contains pictures by Rossetti and Burne-Jones. This village came to mean much to him, and he named his private printing press in London

after it. He also wrote the following, sentimental lines:

'The wind's on the wold and the night is a-cold
And the Thames runs chill twixt mead and hill
But kind and dear is the old house here
And my heart is warm amidst winter's harm.'

LECHLADE

Another town with the peculiar quality that derives more from its rivers, notably the Thames, than from the Cotswolds. In the Middle Ages it was on the Salt Way but Lechlade is very much a river town. At the confluence of three rivers – the Coln, the Leach and the Thames – it was at Lechlade that the stone quarried at Taynton was loaded on to wagons before setting out for London, to be used in the construction of the great St Paul's Cathedral. From 1789 the Thames was linked to the Severn via the Thames and Severn Canal (which started close to here) to the southeast at Inglesham, where the old round house, built for the canal lengthmen (who were responsible for the maintenance of certain lengths of the canal), still stands.

Inevitably, wherever there are rivers there are bridges. Just south of the town, the A361 crosses the Thames with the old toll bridge, the 18th-century Halfpenny (or Ha'penny) Bridge; while to the east the A417 crosses the Thames by means of the 13th-century St John Bridge where a statue of Father Thames presides close to the Thames' highest lock and from where there is a view of the town.

Lechlade is built about its Market Square, and its wool church. The square, and the streets that radiate from it – Burford Street, High Street and St John Street – are overlooked by a collection of fine 17th- to 19th-century buildings. The superb church, with its distinctive spire, dates from the late 15th

century when it was built largely from the same quarries at Taynton that later provided the stone for St Paul's. It contains an east window from 1510 and the brass of wool merchant, John Townsend, as well as a fine chancel roof. One balmy summer evening in 1815 the church inspired the Romantic poet Percy Shelley to write:

'Thou too, aerial pile! Whose pinnacles Point from one shrine like pyramids of fire'

The bustle of commercial river life has long gone from Lechlade, although pleasure craft still bring plenty of colour and movement to the canal and it is possible to hire small boats from the boatyard near the Ha'penny Bridge. The walk along the Thames, southwest from Ha'penny Bridge, is very enjoyable and at Inglesham there is the fine church of St John the Baptist, 30ft (100m) from the river, which was saved by William Morris.

Insight

MORRIS MEMORIAL HALL

Kelmscot's Morris Memorial Hall, the village hall, was designed by Ernest Gimson, an important member of the Arts and Crafts movement, and it was opened by the playwright, George Bernard Shaw in 1933. The site was a gift from Lord Faringdon, while the stone came from the nearby quarry at Filkins, owned by Sir Stafford Cripps, and was similarly offered as a gift. Gimson died before its completion and the work was carried out by a local builder, Mr King of Lechlade.

Just to the southeast of Lechlade is Buscot Park, an 18th-century house, with a well-known series of paintings by Burne-Jones in the saloon, and a trio of Rembrandts among many other works of art reflecting the taste of the 1st Lord Faringdon. The house is set in an attractive, well-laid out park close to the village of Buscot, with its church, and parsonage.

223

Insight

A MACABRE LEGEND

Several legends attach themselves to Minster Lovell Hall. The strangest of all concerns Francis Lovell, a Yorkist, who fled after the Battle of Bosworth, returning in 1487 to champion the cause of the pretender, Lambert Simnel. Defeated at the Battle of Stoke, Lovell returned to the Hall and locked himself in a secret room, attended by a dog and a servant. Somehow, when the servant died, Lovell became trapped in the room and died there. In 1708, during work on the house, a skeleton was apparently discovered seated at a desk, with a dog at its feet.

MINSTER LOVELL

Here is a small village of particular interest. It is, first of all, exceptionally pretty – a fine old bridge spans the Windrush and the main street is lined with an even mixture of Cotswold stone and thatch. Enjoy an entertaining introduction to the village at the Minster Lovell Heritage Centre, just over half a mile (800m) away on the Burford Road.

Park at the far end of the street and walk down to the church. It used to be accompanied by a priory, but it was dissolved in 1414. The remaining church, dedicated to St Kenelm, is quite beautiful. Its beauty is less evident from the outside, but once you go in, the perfection of its design becomes obvious. It is welcoming and comforting, well-tended like a cared-for drawing room, yet uplifting and peaceful. Cruciform in shape, it was built in 1431 on the foundations of an earlier 12th-century church. It lacks only the warming colours of stained-glass windows and some of the other humanising features that have gone in the last few hundred years. But the font is original and the alabaster tomb is thought to belong to William, 7th Baron Lovell, who built the church.

No perfect Cotswold village would be complete without its manor house, of course, and Minster

Lovell's is a beauty, although it is in ruins. The site, in a curve of the river below the church, was picked out by Lord William Lovell in the 1440s. William's son, John, extended the new manor house, and signboards among the broken walls show how splendid it must have been, complete with a massive gatehouse

Sir Thomas Coke, a pioneer of modernised farming techniques, was the last resident at the Hall. He left in 1747 for his new Norfolk home, Holkham Hall. The old house was dismantled and the ruins are now cared for by English Heritage.

Walk through the outline of the ruined Minster Lovell Hall, passing between the spindly tower and the shell of the great hall, to admire the fish ponds. They lie in a tranquil spot below the Church of St Kenelm, shaded by willows and speckled with water lilies. The trout farmed here would have been an important source of food for the Hall, as would the pigeons that lived in the medieval dovecote, open to the public.

A short distance from Minster Lovell, and a pleasant walk along the Windrush River, is the picturesque village of Crawley with a river bridge and an old blanket mill. Just to the south of Minster Lovell lie the Charterville Allotments, the subject of a 19th-century social experiment. The 300 acres (121ha) were purchased by an early socialist and offered as smallholdings to poor families, along with £30 and a pig. The experiment failed but some of the cottages still remain.

THE ROLLRIGHT STONES

These ancient monuments, on the side of the A3400 Stow road not far from Long Compton, consist of two stone circles and a monolith.

The three elements of the Rollright Stones have each been given a name, the King's Men, the Whispering Knights and the King Stone, which derive from a legend explaining their origins. Long ago a band of soldiers met a witch who told them that if their leader were to take seven long strides and 'if Long Compton thou canst see, King of England thou shall be'. The aspiring monarch risked all, saw nothing and was, along with his loyal followers, turned to stone. The Whispering Knights are the traitors who planned to overthrow the king once he became ruler of all England.

The facts are more banal. The 77 King's Men, 100 feet (30.8m) in diameter, and the King Stone, which is probably linked with them in some way, are said to date from 2000–1800 BC, during the Bronze Age; their purpose is uncertain. The Whispering Knights are believed to be the remains of a Neolithic long barrow. The Stones, which can be seen from the A3400, are open to the public, but parking is limited.

The village of Little Rollright has a fine 17th-century manor house and a handsome little church built in the Perpendicular style, which contains some magnificent 17th-century stone monuments. Great Rollright has fine views southwards

Visit

HOOK NORTON

Hook Norton, east of Great Rollright, is known these days, above all, for its beer. Brewed in a Victorian red-brick brewery, Hook Norton Ale is affectionately known as 'Hooky'. Brewery tours are run from their Visitor Centre, which is next door to the village museum. The village's former importance as an ironstone centre is evident from the remains of a huge railway viaduct across the valley.

over rolling countryside. Its historic buildings include the Norman church with its gargoyles and carved doorway. Close by is Wyatt Countryside Centre, where organic food and plants are available.

Not far from the Rollright Stones is Long Compton, strung out along the A3400, an attractive village with a handsome Perpendicular church that you approach through a lychgate, thought to be a cottage with its lower floor removed. The

Rollright Stones are also quite close to the Jurassic Way, a prehistoric route running between the Humber estuary and the southwest of England. That such a route existed suggests a surprising level of contact, and probably trade, between peoples in different areas throughout the country at an early stage in England's history.

SHIPSTON-ON-STOUR

As its name implies, Shipston was an important sheep market town. After the demand for local wool began to decline in the 19th century the town continued to flourish because of the opening of a branch line in 1836 from the horse-drawn tramway that linked Moreton-in-Marsh with Stratford. This line was converted to steam power in 1889. Before that it was an important stop for coaches, and many of the inns in the High Street date from that era.

Around Shipston there are a number of villages that are worth a visit. To the northwest is Ilmington, a delightful scattered village that has a fine manor house and a church that contains work by Robert Thompson, the celebrated early 20th-century furniture maker and craftsman whose signature was always a wooden mouse. To the north is the attractive village of Honington, which is approached by a minor road leading over a five-arched bridge.

Just north of Honington you can find the well-manicured village of Tredington complete with its parish church and fine 15th-century spire. In the porch floor there are the curious fossilised remains of a creature like an ichthyosaurus (a fish lizard). To the south of Shipston is Cherington with a good selection of attractive 18th- and 19th-century houses built of local stone.

SHIPTON-UNDER-WYCHWOOD

Once the neighbour of Bruern Abbey, and once the centre of the Wychwood Forest, Shipton is built about a large village green in the Evenlode Valley.

Visit

TRAGIC VOYAGE

On the green of Shipton-under-Wychwood, close to the Shaven Crown, is a memorial of 1878 erected to 17 parishioners who died in a ship named the Cospatrick which caught fire off Cape Town in 1874 on its way to New Zealand. Tragically, of the 477 passengers presumably aiming to start a new life, only three survived.

At the lower end of the green is St Mary's Church, begun at the end of the 12th century. A fine octagonal spire grows out of its tower, while within the church there is a 14th-century effigy of a woman and a delightful Tudor monument of a family group at prayer.

The uniquely named Shaven Crown Hotel, a handsome stone building close to the green, can trace its history back to 1384 and was run at one time by the Cistercian monks of Bruern Abbey. Bruern was founded in the reign of King Stephen and dissolved in 1536 – nothing now remains. The Shaven Crown, however, once played host to the Fascist leader Oswald Mosley when he was arrested during World War II.

Of Wychwood Forest there is almost nothing left, although it once covered a large area between Stanton Harcourt and Taynton. It was much used by the Normans for hunting and was well known for its deer – indeed the citizens of Burford were entitled to hunt there once each year and the town was entitled to two bucks annually. Most English kings up to Charles I hunted here. In later centuries many of the notable estate parks in the vicinity – Blenheim and Cornbury, for example – were carved out of it and in the centre of the remaining area of forest is a National Nature Reserve, 2 miles (3.2km) east of Shipton.

THE WINDRUSH VALLEY

The Windrush rises at Taddington, near Snowshill, and meanders through many charming Cotswolds

THE WINDRUSH

WINDRUSH VALLEY

Visit

AN ANCIENT DOOR

A curiosity in Sherborne is a cottage at the eastern end of the village. It has a complete Norman doorway, removed, presumably, from the earlier church.

villages already mentioned. Beyond Bourton it widens as it approaches the Thames and continues through a number of villages to the north of the A40, on the borders of Gloucestershire and Oxfordshire. A pleasant walk, the Windrush Way, goes from Winchcombe to Bourton-on-the-Water.

Sherborne, on a tributary of the Windrush, has been for centuries part of the Sherborne estate; before that the land was owned by the Abbots of Winchcombe, whose sheep were sheared on the banks of the river every summer. Sherborne House, allegedly haunted by its former owner, John 'Crump' Dutton, the Royalist hunchback, was rebuilt

in the 19th century. Occupied by the military during World War II, it then became a boarding school. It now belongs to the National Trust and, although it is not open to the public, there are waymarked walks through the woods and parkland. Lodge Park, an elaborate grandstand for deer-coursing in the 17th century, is open to the public.

The next village to the east is Windrush with a church topped by a fine Perpendicular tower and a magnificent Norman south doorway surrounded by beakheads, bird-like grotesques of mysterious origin. Then come the Barringtons, first Little, then Great, once renowned for their stone quarries and the local families of masons, the Kempsters and the Strongs, who worked them. No evidence remains of the old subterranean quarries and Little Barrington is a quiet little village, its cottages very prettily clustered about its village green. The Fox Inn nearby, is by a bridge over the river, built by local master mason Thomas

Strong, principal contractor of St Paul's and regarded by Christopher Wren as the leading builder of the day. Great Barrington, to the north, has a Norman church with some fine monuments by the 18th-century sculptor Joseph Nollekens, while the country house and landscaped gardens of Barrington Park are to the east of it.

East of Great Barrington lies Taynton, another village that once supplied London and Oxford with its famous prime building stone – taken from open-cast quarries, it was transported overland to Lechlade and thence by barge to London. Beyond it is Burford and then Widford church, the poignant remains of a once thriving village that simply disappeared, probably as a result of the plague. The 13th-century church, built on the site of a Roman villa, stands small and solitary on a raised mound overlooking the river, and is worth a look for its box pews, and 14th-century wall paintings.

A short way from Widford is Swinbrook, a village associated with the Mitford family, particularly five of Lord Redesdale's daughters, Nancy, Diana, Unity, Jessica and Deborah. Unity became a close friend of Adolf Hitler, Diana married the British fascist leader, Sir Oswald Mosley, Deborah became the Duchess of Devonshire, while Nancy and Jessica became well-known writers. Nancy, Pamela, Diana and Unity are buried in the graveyard of the church, which contains the wonderful triple-decker monument to the Fettiplace family who once owned a mansion here. Across the river to the southeast is Asthall, a charming village with a fine Elizabethan manor.

WITNEY

Another Windrush town, Witney remains famous for its blankets, the production of which somehow managed to survive the collapse of the Cotswold woollen industry after the Industrial Revolution. The Market Square is the centre of the town and

contains an unusual Butter Cross, refurbished in the 19th century, and the 17th-century Town Hall. Beyond, near a green, is the 13th-century church, complete with its massive tower, and a fine collection of houses that date from the 17th and 18th centuries. The town's museum is in Gloucester Court Mews in the High Street. Also in the High Street you will see the Blanket Hall, built in 1721 by the Company of Blanket Weavers, a group of prosperous weavers who were granted their charter in 1711.

Just to the southeast of Witney, and well-signposted on the A40, is the Cogges Manor Farm Museum, reflecting farming life in the Edwardian period. Among the machinery and livestock, you will find a working kitchen and dairy.

WOODSTOCK

A small town of some charm, most famous as the home of the Churchill family, whose ancestral home is Blenheim Palace. It has enjoyed

Visit

WIDFORD CHURCH

This isolated church at Widford is of mainly 13th-century origin and has some interesting wall paintings that date from the 14th-century. The tiny church takes its name from St Oswald, the Saxon King of Northumbria who was killed in battle in ad 642 by Penda of Mercia. It is thought that the church owes its precise location to the fact that the saint's body was rested here on its way to burial at Gloucester.

royal patronage since Henry I built an extensive park and hunting lodge here in the 12th century, which his grandson, Henry II, preferred to use to entertain his mistress, the fair Rosamund. The lodge became a palace and the town grew around it. The medieval author of *The Canterbury Tales* and *Troilus and Criseyde*, Geoffrey Chaucer, lived in Woodstock for some years, while in later centuries the town was noted for its glovemaking.

Insight

A DEMANDING EMPLOYER

A prodigious display of ill feeling, in keeping with the magnitude of the undertaking, sadly accompanied the construction of Blenheim Palace. The design is the work of Sir John Vanbrugh (who also built Castle Howard in Yorkshire) but in Sarah Jennings, the wife of the Duke of Marlborough, he found himself in the hands of a demanding employer whose capricious nature finally led him to resign the commission in 1716, fortunately after most of the work had been accomplished. Although Nicholas Hawksmoor oversaw the final construction, it was, however, largely the Duchess' tenacity that ensured completion of the building after the death of her husband – not only did she find the money when Queen Anne's government failed to stump up all the promised funds, she was also responsible for much of the interior design.

Woodstock palace remained a favourite with the royal family until 1704 when the manor was presented to John Churchill, First Duke of Marlborough after his success against the French at the Battle of Blenheim. The medieval buildings were subsequently replaced with the magnificent pile that we see today, and christened Blenheim Palace.

Designed by John Vanbrugh, it is perhaps the greatest palace in England, its Baroque extravagance brilliantly humanised by the beauty of the 2,000-acre (810ha) park, landscaped by 'Capability' Brown. The beauty of the relationship between the palace and its grounds can best be appreciated by walking from the town and entering the park through Nicholas Hawksmoor's Triumphal Arch, or the Woodstock Gate, just off Park Street. Merely to walk around the palace, cross the Grand Bridge and enjoy the views as you walk to the Column of Victory, is breathtaking, but you can also enjoy the rose garden, the Butterfly

House, where you can see exotic butterflies, and the Marlborough maze, the world's largest symbolic hedge maze.

The palace itself is replete with gilt and grandeur – carvings by Grinling Gibbons, Flemish tapestries illustrating the martial valour of the duke, and a fine collection of paintings. In the Great Hall is the magnificent ceiling painted by Sir James Thornhill, while the Long Library is one of the longest single rooms in Britain. The first duke and duchess are buried in the chapel, which was built by Hawksmoor in 1731. The room where Sir Winston Churchill was born is the focal point of an exhibition devoted to his life.

The town of Woodstock itself is worthy of some exploration. The streets that cluster around the 18th-century Town Hall are lined with a fine assortment of houses and inns from the 17th and 18th centuries. The most famous is the Bear Hotel, which dates back to the 13th century. The Parish Church of St

Activity

PALATIAL PLAYGROUND

The grounds of Blenheim offer other distractions – there is a children's playground and you can hire rowing boats on Blenheim Lake to go fishing. The park is also the venue for events such as craft fairs, horse trials and even jousting, throughout the year.

Mary Magdalen is set in a charming churchyard and is surmounted by a classical tower of 1785. The Norman south doorway is particularly fine.

Opposite the church, in Park Street, is Fletcher's House. Originally built for a 17th-century merchant, it now houses the Oxfordshire Museum, with galleries and exhibitions about the fascinating history and traditions of Oxfordshire. The museum has a convenient small café and bookshop. The elegant town house also has pleasant gardens. The town stocks are preserved at the museum entrance.

243

TOURIST INFORMATION CENTRES

Burford
The Brewery, Sheep Street.
Tel: 01993 823558

Chipping Norton
The Guildhall, Goddards Lane.
Tel: 01608 644379

Witney
Town Hall, Market Square.
Tel: 01993 775802

Woodstock
Oxford County Museum,
Park Street.
Tel: 01993 813276

PLACES OF INTEREST

Blenheim Palace
Woodstock.
Tel: 0870 060 2080;
www.blenheimpalace.com

Chipping Norton Museum
High Street, Chipping Norton.
Tel: 01608 641712

**Churchill and Sarsden Heritage
Centre**
Churchill Old Church,
Hastings Hill, Churchill.
Tel: 01608 658603

Cogges Manor Farm Museum
Church Lane, Witney.
Tel: 01993 772602;
www.cogges.org

Cotswold Wildlife Park
Burford.
Tel: 01993 823006;
www.cotswoldwildlifepark.co.uk

Hook Norton Brewery Visitor Centre
Brewery Lane, Hook Norton.
Tel: 01608 730384;
www.hooknortonbrewery.co.uk

Kelmscott Manor
Kelmscot.
Tel: 01367 252486;
www.kelmscottmanor.co.uk

Minster Lovell Hall and Dovecot
Minster Lovell.
Tel: 0870 333 1181;
www.english-heritage.org.uk

Minster Lovell Heritage Centre
130 Burford Road, Minster Lovell.
Tel: 01993 775262;
www.minsterlovell.com

North Leigh Roman Villa
North Leigh.
Tel: 0870 331 1181;
www.english-heritage.org.uk

Oxfordshire Museum
Fletcher House, Park Street,
Woodstock.
Tel: 01993 811456;
www.oxfordshire.gov.uk
Swinford Museum of Rural Life
Filkins. Tel: 01367 860209
Tolsey Museum
High Street, Burford.
Tel: 01993 823196;
www.tolseymuseumburford.com
Witney and District Museum
Gloucester Court Mews, High Street,
Witney. Tel: 01993 775915
Wyatt's Countryside Centre
Great Rollright.
Tel: 01608 684835

SHOPPING

The main shopping areas are
Charlbury, Chipping Norton (market,
Wed), Burford, Witney.
Chipping Norton
Farmers' Market, third Sat, Market
Square.
Witney
Farmers' Market, third Thu and Sat,
Church Green.

LOCAL SPECIALITIES
Wool
Cotswold Woollen Weavers, Filkins.
Tel: 01367 860491;
www.naturalbest.co.uk

PERFORMING ARTS
Chipping Norton Theatre
Spring Street, Chipping Norton.
Tel: 01608 642350;
www.chippingnortontheatre.co.uk

SPORTS & ACTIVITIES
HORSE-RIDING
Nether Westcote
Overdale Equestrian Centre.
Tel: 01993 832520

ANNUAL EVENTS & CUSTOMS
Burford
Dragon Procession, Jun.
Great Barrington
Gloucestershire Guild of Craftsmen
Spring Exhibition, May/Jun.

245

TEA ROOMS

Huffkins
98 High Street, Burford, OX18 4QF
Tel: 01993 822126
www.huffkins.com
A wonderful range of freshly made
speciality bread and cakes is on sale
here, with tempting sandwiches and
home-made soup as well. In addition to
the tea room, there is a shop.

Hill Barn Farm Tea Room
Hill Barn Farm, Great Rollright,
Nr Chipping Norton, OX7 5SH
Tel: 01608 684835
Part of a popular farm shop, this
spacious and very clean tea room is
justifiably popular. Anything from light
lunches to mouthwatering teas can be
enjoyed throughout the year.

Daylesford Organic
Daylesford, Nr Kingham, GL56 0YG
Tel: 01608 731700
www.daylesfordorganic.com
Enjoy organic hand-made bread and
pastries at this beautifully designed
café. There's also a farm shop,
a shop selling clothes and homewares.
There's even a yoga studio with a lovely
rural view.

Harriet's
20 High Street, Woodstock, OX20 1TF
Tel: 01993 811231
The finest continental-style croissants,
cakes and patisseries are made here
by a Frenchman, and most of the other
food, such as the clotted cream and the
honey, comes from local producers.

The Bull Inn
Sheep Street, Charlbury,
OX7 3RR
Tel: 01608 810689
www.bullinn-charlbury.com
Low beams, inglenook fireplaces
and scrubbed wood floors create the
appropriate atmosphere in this 16th-
century coaching inn. Outside, the
vine-covered terrace is the ideal place
to enjoy the sunshine.

The Crown Inn
Mill Lane, Church Enstone, OX7 4NN
Tel: 01608 677262
www.crowninnenstone.co.uk
Run by an award-winning chef, this
17th-century stone inn is comfortable
and welcoming. They specialise in
fresh fish; all the food comes from
local suppliers and is delicious. There
is also a picturesque cottage garden.

The Five Alls
Filkins, GL7 3JQ
Tel: 01367 860306
www.thefivealls.co.uk
Just down the road from the Cotswold
Woollen Weavers, this 18th-century
pub offers a wide range of good food in
a bright, welcoming bar, with scrubbed
wooden tables and terracotta walls.
Games for children are provided in the
garden at the back.

The Fox
Great Barrington, Nr Burford,
OX18 4TB
Tel: 01451 844385
www.foxinnbarrington.co.uk
Idyllically situated on the banks of the
River Windrush, this is a perfect place
to unwind. The pretty patio and beer
garden look down on the river, while
inside there are old beams and real
fires. There is an inventive menu and
good local beers.

USEFUL INFORMATION

OTHER INFORMATION
English Heritage
29 Queen Square, Bristol.
Tel: 0117 975 0700;
www.english-heritage.org.uk
National Trust
Severn Region, Mythe End House,
Tewkesbury.
Tel: 01684 850051
www.nationaltrust.org.uk
Wildlife Trust
Tel: 01452 383333
www.gloucestershirewildlifetrust.co.uk
Parking
Park with care in small villages
which have no car parks and take
care not to block driveways or field
entrances. If you park on the road,
allow room for vehicles, including
lorries, to pass.

Places of interest
We give details of just some of the
places to visit within the area covered
by this guide. Further information
can be obtained from local tourist
information centres or the internet.
Weather Call
For details of weather conditions in
Wiltshire, Gloucestershire and Avon.
Tel: 09068 500405
Cycling
The website for the Cotswold District
Council (www.cotswold.gov.uk/
nqcontent) has downloadable cycling
routes on quiet lanes and farm tracks
and also has details on where to hire
bikes. *Pub Walks & Cycle Rides in the
Cotswolds*, from AA Publishing, has
forty mapped and family-friendly walks
and cycle rides.

Walking

For further information on the 100-mile long Cotswold Way National Trail, see www.nationaltrail.co.uk/Cotswold

Birdwatching

For information on the Wildfowl & Wetlands Trust centre at Slimbridge in Gloucestershire, visit www.wwt.org.uk/visit/slimbrige

Public Transport

A great website for public transport is the Cotswolds Area of Outstanding Natural Beauty site at www.cotswoldsaonb.com Under the heading 'Transport' you'll find bus and train timetables for each of the Cotswolds.

Fishing

The Cotswold Water Park in South Cerney has numerous lakes where you can go fishing. Visit the website www.waterpark.org/leisure/angling.html

INDEX

INDEX

ACKNOWLEDGEMENTS

The Automobile Association would like to thank the following photographers, companies and picture libraries for their assistance in the preparation of this book.

Abbreviations for the picture credits are as follows – (t) top; (b) bottom; (c) centre; (l) left; (r) right; (AA) AA World Travel Library.

2/3 AA/H Palmer; 5 AA/H Palmer; 6 AA/D Hall; 9 AA/S Day; 12/3 AA/D Hall; 14 AA/D Hall;15t AA/D Hall; 15b AA/D Hall; 16 AA/S Day; 17 AA/H Palmer; 19 AA/S Day; 20 AA/D Hall; 23 AA/M Birkitt; 24/5 AA/D Hall; 26 AA/D Hall; 28/9 AA/S Day; 30 AA/S Day; 31t AA/H Palmer; 31b AA/S Day; 32 AA/D Hall; 34/5 AA/R Rainford; 37 AA/D Hall; 38 AA/D Hall; 41 AA/H Palmer; 42/3 AA/T Souter; 45 AA/D Hall; 46 AA/S Day; 49 AA/D Hall; 50 AA/D Hall; 53 AA/D Hall; 54/5 AA/S Day; 56 AA/D Hall; 59 AA/N Ray; 60 AA/S Day; 63 AA/D Hall; 64 AA/D Hall; 67 AA/D Hall; 68 AA/S Day; 75 AA/D Hall; 76 AA/D Hall; 78 AA/D Hall; 80/1 AA/S Day; 82 AA/D Hall; 83t AA/H Palmer; 83b AA/D Hall; 85 AA/D Hall; 86 AA/H Palmer; 89 AA/H Palmer; 90/1 AA/H Palmer; 92 AA/H Palmer; 95 AA/S Day; 96 AA/H Palmer; 98/9 AA/S Day; 100 AA/S & O Mathews; 103 AA/H Palmer; 104 AA/E Meacher; 106/7 AA/D Hall;109 AA/D Hall; 110/11 AA/S Day; 112 AA/D Hall; 115 AA/C Jones; 116 AA/P Baker; 123 AA/P Baker; 124 AA/D Hall;126 AA/D Hall; 128/9 AA/S Day; 130 AA/S & O Mathews; 131 AA/S Day; 132 AA/K Doran; 133 AA/J Wyand; 134 AA/M Birkitt; 137 AA/M Birkitt; 138/9 AA/S Day;140 AA/S Day;143 AA/E Meacher; 146 AA/H Palmer; 149 AA/D Hall; 150 AA/D Hall; 155 AA/S Day;156 AA/S Day; 159 AA/S Day; 160 A/D Hall; 162/3 AA/S Day; 166/7 AA/S Day; 169 AA/D Hall; 170 AA/D Hall; 175 AA/D Hall; 178 AA/D Hall; 182/3 AA/S Day; 185 AA/D Hall; 191 AA/D Hall; 192 AA/D Hall; 194 AA/S Day; 196/7 AA/S Day; 198 AA/C Jones; 199t AA/R Rainford; 199b AA/S Day; 200 AA/D Hall; 203 AA/S Day; 204 AA/D Hall; 207 AA/D Hall; 210/11 AA/S Day; 212 AA/K Doran; 214/5 AA/D Hall; 216 AA/S Day; 218/9 AA/D Hall; 221 AA/S Day; 222 AA/M Short; 225 AA/D Hall; 226/7 AA/D Hall; 230 AA/D Hall; 233 AA/K Doran; 234/5 AA/D Hall; 238 AA/S Day; 241 AA/D Hall; 242 AA/C Jones; 247 AA/D Hall; 248 AA/D Hall.

Every effort has been made to trace the copyright holders, and we apologise in advance for any accidental errors. We would be happy to apply the corrections in the following edition of this publication.